Praise for Win-Win for the Greater Good

"*Win-Win for the Greater Good* provides the 'how to' blueprint for organizations of any size and from any sector to build highly productive partnerships. It reveals the true essence of success - focusing on the business objectives of your partner, while striving together to create a greater good."

Casey Sheahan, CEO, Patagonia, Inc.

"*Win-Win* lucidly captures Bruce Burtch's decades of practitioner wisdom on cross-sector partnerships. The book is filled with rich examples and insightful practical guidance on how to build powerful partnerships. Read it and learn from a master!"

James E. Austin, Eliot I. Snider and Family Professor of Business Administration, Emeritus, Harvard Business School, Author, *The Collaboration Challenge*

"A 'must read' for any organization. Through real stories and his deep experience, Bruce Burtch proves that magic can happen when a partnership is focused on creating a greater good."

Howard Behar, President, Starbucks Coffee International, Retired

"America had Christopher Columbus. Cause marketing has Bruce Burtch. A man of firsts like the great explorer, Bruce has been designing innovative, highly-successful cross-sector partnerships since 1975. *Win-Win for the Greater Good* will help you chart a course for success for your organization and for a better world."

Joe Waters, Selfishgiving.com, Co-author, *Cause Marketing for Dummies*

"If you are looking for a guidebook on how to best ignite your organization's economic and social impact on your stakeholders, your community and our world... this is it!"

Chip Conley, Founder of Joie de Vivre Hospitality and Author of *PEAK*

"In *Win-Win for the Greater Good* Bruce Burtch takes over three decades of first-hand experience and puts it into an easy-to-follow, step-by-step guidebook for the creation of successful cross-sector partnerships. Bruce gave in-depth partnership training to 85 nonprofit organizations sponsored by Autodesk. The response from attendees was enthusiastic and very positive. I recommend Bruce's book to nonprofit or for-profit organizations wishing to stimulate their community engagement and effectiveness."

Julie Wilder, Manager of Employee Impact Programs, Autodesk

"An amazing compilation of great ideas! *Win-Win for the Greater Good* provides terrific tools and concepts that will help your non-profit, your business or your community make a difference in the lives of many."

Sherri Lewis Wood, Founder, One Warm Coat

"Worth its weight in fundraising gold. *Win-Win for the Greater Good* turns the tables on traditional approaches to nonprofit/for-profit funding relationships. It challenges you to build a business value proposition and provides over 30 ways to beneficially impact your organization through partnerships, while greatly increasing your service impact."

Peggy Duvette, Executive Director, WiserEarth

"Best book ever written on this important subject! A treasure chest of ideas for creating good."

Mary O'Mara, Executive Director, Marinlink

"I've had the privilege of seeing Bruce utilize the concepts and 'how to' steps contained in this book with extraordinary results in the work he has done with us at Ramsell. If you're a for-profit or not-for-profit looking for ways to develop or enhance cross-sector partnerships, I believe you'll find this book to be a tremendous resource to help you accomplish your goals."

Tim Murrill, Executive Vice President, Sales & Marketing, Ramsell

"Anyone seriously interested in developing a cross-sector partnership and exceling at it must read this stimulating and thought-provoking book from someone that has dedicated his life to this field."

Solomon Belette, CEO, Catholic Charities of the East Bay

"Where is it written that giving back to the community should only benefit the recipient and not the giver? Thank you, Bruce for dispensing with that myth so effectively. (And, hopefully once and for all!) And you do better than that - you demonstrate how the collaboration of businesses with non-profits exponentially produces benefits to an entire community. This book should be the 'go to' reference for company executives, small business owners and leaders of non-profits."

Vicki Whiting, Publisher, *Kid Scoop News*

"Bruce Burtch was born to be the guru of nonprofit/for-profit partnerships having worked for both types of organizations, large and small, in management and on the front lines. He truly understands the clashing forces that can make or break organizations, appreciates the nuances that can bring them together or push them apart, and knows how to harness the collective win-win potential of partnerships between organizations from different sectors of business that didn't realize – until he showed them the way – their mutual needs."

J. David Pincus, Ph.D, Author and Visiting Professor, University of Arkansas

"Bruce Burtch's message is both powerful and pragmatic. With clear step-by-step direction enriched by real-life examples, *Win-Win for the Greater Good* is an essential read for any organization that wants to extend its reach, optimize limited resources . . . and fulfill its mission."

Rick Knapp, Retired business executive, Consultant, Non-profit board member

WIN-WIN

for the Greater Good

The step-by-step guidebook on
creating partnerships that will ignite
your for-profit or nonprofit organization's
revenue, reputation and social impact
while creating a greater good for society

Bruce W. Burtch

DEDICATION PAGE

It's My Father's Fault

From the very beginning, all I ever saw in my father was a man committed deeply to giving back to his community for the blessings he had been given - "paying his dues" he called it. No matter what challenge life threw at him, he never turned away, never complained, never stopped helping one more charitable organization, one more person who needed a hand. If I have ever done anything in my life that has helped others, I must blame my father. As my role model he stands above all others and I thank the good Lord for giving me, and so many others, a man who lives by his personal motto: Life is Good. And so is he.

ACKNOWLEDGEMENTS

Many people have had a hand in developing this book. First and foremost, I want to thank my wife Janie for her patience over the years through my endless search for save-the-world ideas. Writing this guidebook on building cross-sector partnerships and cause marketing was one project she strongly supported, as she knew that what I have experienced in 35 years - developing partnerships focused on creating a greater good - was an important message to share.

To three dear friends - David Pincus, Rick Knapp and Steve Wood - who offered not only strong encouragement to write the book but who also took on the arduous task of reviewing its initial draft. Each of them is a consummate professional, extraordinarily smart and with gentle yet firm criticism.

To Alison Owings, my editor, whose revisions made me really pleased with what I wrote! She was and is simply amazing.

To my guest contributors, Ed Chansky, Bob Lanier and Farron Levy, who are players at the very top of their game and who without a blink, offered their expertise. Their contributions brought great insight into areas I would not dare to venture alone.

To James E. Austin, Eliot I. Snider and Family Professor of Business Administration, Emeritus, Harvard Business School, Author, *The Collaboration Challenge*, for his support of this book and inspirational work in the field of collaboration.

To Dr. William Ury, co-author of the landmark work, *Getting to Yes: Negotiating Agreement Without Giving In*, for kindly reviewing and approving what I wrote in this book.

To my colleague Joe Waters, who lent his review and expertise in cause marketing, proving it somewhat ironic that he co-wrote the book, *Cause Marketing for Dummies*, which only someone as smart as Joe could write so well.

To Brian Narelle, for the amazing cartoons and characters that flow from his always-churning, most creative mind. He has given this story its leading character, Glow, and so much more.

To Christie Kragel, my multi-talented stepdaughter, who undertook the arduous task of copyediting the final manuscript - a job very well done!

And finally, to all the friends, colleagues and clients from the nonprofit, for-profit, education and government sectors with whom I have traveled this journey so far and shared the goal of making a difference.

Thank you all.

CONTENTS

WIN-WIN RESOURCE CENTER

To assist your development of cross-sector partnerships and cause marketing, I have provided a companion online Win-Win **Resource Center**. Here you will find extensive research on cross-sector partnerships and cause marketing, PDFs, forms, templates, articles from our contributing experts, presentations, videos and other valuable and continually updated material.

Free access to all this information can be found: *www.bruceburtch.com/ResourceCenter.*

WHY I WROTE THIS GUIDEBOOK

Having spent more than 35 years deep in the trenches of developing cross-sector partnerships and cause marketing campaigns with the non-profit, for-profit, education and government sectors, I have learned what works and what doesn't. I have developed partnerships - from a local two-person art program, a three county children's magazine, regional campaigns for Fortune 500 corporations to cause marketing for an international sports organization, and all sizes and variations in between. I have experienced people in all types of organizations working together. And through it, all I have developed a step-by-step, proven process to planning and implementing successful cross-sector partnerships.

Beginning with my first job at Cedar Point in Sandusky, Ohio, the world's largest pure amusement park, where I developed a relationship with the state-sponsored Ohio Travel Council, I discovered the many benefits of bringing different sectors together in a mutually rewarding relationship. A few years later, I was hired by Marriott Corporation as Public Affairs Manager and given the task (at age 25) to design the opening promotion of its largest project in history: the family entertainment center Marriott's Great America in Santa Clara, California. It was here where I conceived and directed my first comprehensive cross-sector partnership campaign with the March of Dimes. Through the challenges, opportunities and understanding gained through this relationship, the main theme of my career was set: cross-sector partnerships provide more benefit to all the partners than each could have ever accomplished alone.

From those early experiences and beyond, in my work as Public Relations Director of the United States Olympic Committee, to the founding of The William Bentley Agency, an integrated public relations/marketing agency, to the honor of serving as director of market-

A cross-sector partnership is a multifaceted, value-driven relationship between two or more partners from the nonprofit, for-profit, education or government sectors, focused on creating a greater good for society.

ing & communications for the American Red Cross (San Francisco) Bay Area chapter, to my current role as Founder/CEO of Bruce W. Burtch, Inc., a cross-sector partnership consulting and training firm, each role and relationship along this path have created a foundation of knowledge that I wanted to share.

I wrote this guidebook because I have seen thousands of organizations from all sectors struggling through the recent economic times. I have seen and still see a lot of pain and a need for help and real answers. Yet I know from experience that there is an extraordinary amount of opportunity lying in wait for the right combination of partners, on any issue, in any sector, in any small town or metropolitan city, in any corner of the world. Cross-sector partnerships can be extraordinarily successful when these partners join together for their individual and mutual success, while focusing on creating benefit for the greater good.

What I hadn't found was a comprehensive course or "how to" guidebook on the development of cross-sector partnerships. And while the principles and practices presented in this book will benefit any size organization from any sector, my primary focus is small to midsize organizations - roughly speaking, those with between 10 and 500 employees. This is a vast market with approximately 2,000,000 nonprofit and for-profit organizations in the United States alone falling within this employment range. This does not include the tens of thousands of educational institutions, school districts and governmental agencies. It is with these "smaller" organizations where I have found cross-sector partnerships to be the least utilized and consequently, where I feel there is enormous opportunity to stimulate their economic and social benefit success, and thus improve the overall economy and well-being of our country and many others.

Two other activities also fueled my desire to better understand and share the information I had learned. First, as National Writer on cross-sector partnerships and cause marketing for *Examiner.com*, an online news service which reaches 242 markets across the United States and Canada, I have had the opportunity to interview many executives from the nonprofit, for-profit, education and government sectors. Many of these interviews were published in my on-going series, Profiles in Partnership. And secondly, my company undertakes an annual survey, *The Burtch Report*, which provides a detailed analysis of cross-sector partnerships involving small to midsize nonprofit and for-profit organizations. These two activities have provided exceptional access to thought leaders and an understanding of the opportunities and challenges facing smaller organizations.

Win-Win for the Greater Good is a guidebook, not an overview, not a nice collection of stories. My goal is to take over three decades of experience in developing partnerships between all sectors and provide you with the blueprint, the materials and the tools that will guide you in developing highly successful, highly profitable cross-sector partnerships. Here you will find information from the very basic to more challenging concepts. Each reader comes to this guidebook with different experiences and different levels of expertise.

In 1978, I was asked by the president of a large foundation what I wanted to do with my life, and almost without thinking I said, "I want to do well by doing good". He leaned back in his chair, laughed heartedly and replied, "I've never seen anybody do that before." That very phrase to "do well by doing good" has been my personal mantra and foundation of my work from that minute forward. From the bottom of my heart I believe that doing good is the necessary prerequisite for doing well. Doing good benefits everything you do and everything you are. Doing good and doing well can best be accomplished through win-win partnerships.

And that's why I wrote this book.

Bruce W. Burtch

SOCCER BALLS

All we wanted were 10 soccer balls.

It was 1979 and I was a volunteer with the San Francisco Special Olympics. One of our athletes was Joey and Joey had down-syndrome. He was about as round and he was tall, and he was always running, always smiling, always coming up to me saying, "Coach, what are we doing next?" Very special people like Joey are why I wanted to be part of Special Olympics. And Joey wanted to play soccer. But we didn't have a soccer program. We realized that soccer would be one of the easiest sports that could reach almost all of our athletes, and at very little cost. We had free use of sports fields, all of our athletes had some form of a running or tennis shoe and we had volunteers with some background in soccer. All we needed were the soccer balls – about ten dollars each.

Like any nonprofit, we didn't want to pay for anything we could otherwise get donated, so we connected with a friend who worked in the Community Relations Department at San Francisco-based Levi Strauss & Co. We asked her if Levi's would donate $100 to buy 10 soccer balls for our new program.

Levi's agreed and the first Special Olympics soccer program in northern California was born. And Joey was ecstatic.

We soon realized, however, that we didn't have enough volunteers to handle the number of athletes now interested in playing soccer. We then went back to Levi's and asked if they might have some volunteers to help us.

They did and our soccer program grew even more.

Levi's Employee Relations Department took notice of this enthusiasm from their employees and wrote an article in the company newsletter. That brought not only greater recognition to our program but even more volunteers. Then a local newspaper did a story on this burgeoning relationship between Levi's and Special Olympics. In time, one of Levi's executives joined our Board of Directors. Levi was also becoming one of the largest financial supporters of our Special Olympics program.

Meanwhile, apart from being a board member of San Francisco Special Olympics, my day job was Director of Public Relations for the United States Olympic Committee. I was gearing up for the 1980 Olympic Summer Games in Moscow. But the Cold War was getting hotter, Russia invaded Afghanistan, and because of that, President Jimmy Carter announced that the United States was boycotting the Olympic Games. From this huge disappointment came a surprise gift.

Fred Banks, then president of Levi's Women's Wear division, called me up. He said, "Bruce as you certainly know, Levi's was the official team outfitter for the U.S. Olympic team and because we are not going to the Olympic Games we have all of the official U.S. Olympic Team uniforms and warm-ups. We cannot sell or use them in any commercial manner, and they're just sitting in a warehouse." Then Fred said the most amazing thing: "Would you be interested in Levi's donating these Olympic Team uniforms to Special Olympics?" After I picked myself up off the floor, we discussed the logistics.

One of the most moving experiences imaginable is watching Special Olympics athletes enter a stadium for their games. Every athlete is brimming with pride and excitement. Now imagine that following summer at stadiums across the country, Special Olympics athletes making their entrance while wearing the official uniforms of the 1980 United States Olympic team, emblazoned with a large USA across the back. To everyone involved, it was a magical, emotional moment.

The relationship between the Special Olympics and Levi's kept growing. It certainly helped the Special Olympics. But in terms of positive media coverage, employee morale and much more, it also helped Levi's.

And it all started with 10 soccer balls.

As we fast-forward, it is abundantly clear that we live in a challenging time. In 2011 the Chronicle of Philanthropy reported that the nation's largest charities saw a decline of 11% in donations, greater than any in the past 20 years. And while some indications show that nonprofit funding is turning around, according to "Giving USA," charitable giving grew less than one percent in 2012. Thousands of smaller nonprofit organizations are at high risk of closing down. This sad situation comes at a time when there is increasing demand for the social services these organizations provide.

The social support system is in trouble and those people it supports have nowhere to turn. Anne Wilson, CEO of the United Way of the San Francisco Bay Area, warned "the recession has severely compromised our community's safety net." As a moral public, we cannot let this safety net fail.

However, individual, corporate and foundation funders impacted by the decline of their income, sales or investment portfolios cannot, in many cases, maintain their past support levels when there is so much need. Tough decisions must be made - who to support and at what level. The desire to help must be tempered by financial reality.

The situation is serious and for many, this is entirely new territory. The time has passed for believing we can operate as we always have under "normal" circumstances because "normal" doesn't exist anymore. The answers do not come from staying the course. The answers come in the realization that to weather this storm, the nonprofit, for-profit, education and government sectors must find new approaches, proven techniques and new economic streams that will work, even in these challenging times.

The organizations that will lead the new normal are the ones that realize they need not and should not take on these challenges alone. As in the soccer ball story, there are astonishing opportunities for organizations that collaborate, indeed partner, with organizations in other sectors. These organizations will lead their industry and their community in doing good. These are the organizations and people who will attract the most publicity, drive new sales or donations, increase their brand recognition and create the greatest goodwill.

The management of these more enlightened organizations are not afraid to share and not afraid to partner with other sectors. They're not the ones who work in silos, treasuring their own personal power rather than the much greater power of the collective body. They will stand firm against those afraid of this new collaborative thinking. The irony is that the leaders and organizations who want to stay the course may lose market share and profitability, may demoralize employees and all stakeholders by their myopic focus on their organization and their bottom-line.

This is not a time for business as usual. Now is the time to take full advantage of multi-benefit cross-sector partnerships focused on the greater good. This is the new normal and it's win-win.

PART I

GOOD TO GREAT TO GLOWING

In Jim Collins' book, *Good to Great*, he described a "great" company as one company whose financial performance achieved several multiples better than the stock market average over a sustained period. He also attributed the main factor for achieving this greatness as having a company focus its resources on its particular field of competence. Much has changed since this was published in 2001, especially the fast rising tide of consumer concern, and in some cases, demand for the business community to be more focused on sustainability, being good citizens, and giving back to their communities.

In *Good to Great*, Collins identifies 11 companies (Gillette, Kroger, Walgreens, Wells Fargo, Phillip Morris and others) he felt had made this transition from good to great. The standard he used was that these companies had either met or underperformed the stock market for a 15 year period and then transitioned to providing returns of at least three times that of the stock market over the subsequent period.

In *Firms of Endearment* published in 2007, authors Raj Sisodia, Jag Sheth and David B. Wolfe, challenged the more traditional capitalistic understanding as to what is seen as being a successful business. Their book promotes the need for a "new capitalism of caring" with its focus that all stakeholders must be equally valued. This approach mirrored my own beliefs and experience that there was a much better way for corporations to benefit everyone involved with their organization, both internally and externally, and not just their shareholders.

The authors of *Firms of Endearment* took a very different path in their analysis. Their research sought out companies that strived to "endear" themselves to all their stakeholder groups—customers, employees, partners, communities, and shareholders. They looked for companies that aligned the interests of all stakeholders in such a way that no stakeholder group gains at the expense of other stakeholder groups.

The companies they selected included Amazon, BMW, The Container Store, eBay, Google, Patagonia, Southwest Airlines, Starbucks, Whole Foods and others.

When the authors of *Firms of Endearment* completed their analysis of just the one category of stock market performance and the return to investors during the period of 1996 to 2006 (the primary focus of *Good to Great*, they found that:

1) Over a 10-year horizon, *Firms of Endearment* companies out performed the Good to Great companies by 1026% to 331% (a 3.1 to 1 ratio).

2) Over five years, *Firms of Endearment* companies outperformed Good to Great companies by 128% to 77% (a 1.7 to 1 ratio).

3) Over three years, *Firms of Endearment* companies performed on par with Good to Great companies 73% to 75%.

By focusing on the benefits to all stakeholders, the *Firms of Endearment* companies met, or in the five and 10 year periods, greatly outperformed companies that focused primarily on stock performance and return to investors. This message cannot be emphasized enough. The authors summed up this comparison by saying that they had a "seismic disagreement" with *Good to Great* when it comes to defining what is "great." They concluded, "To us, a great company is one that makes the world a better place because it exists, not simply a company that outperforms the market by a certain percentage over a certain period of time."

Glowing Your Business

No matter what kind of work you do, you are in business. Whether you are a sole consultant, run a small hardware store, or are the CEO of a Fortune 500 corporation, you are in business. You may be Executive Director or run fund development for a nonprofit organization, teach in your local elementary school or work in an agency of state government, whatever the case, you are in business. A business can be defined as an occupation, profession, calling, vocation or employment. In other words, if you are in any sector of for-profit, nonprofit, education or government, you are in business. So the vast majority of what you find in this book will relate to your work in any sector.

However, when I talk about this desired transformation of "glowing your business," I'm referring to the for-profit sector. The basic premise of this book is that a for-profit organization can only glow when it has joined hand-in-hand in partnership with one or more from the nonprofit, education or government sectors to create a greater good.

This brings us to what I feel is the next step in the evolution, and potentially revolution, of business: going from a good company to a great company to a glowing company. You become a glowing company when you have purposefully embedded a "cause consciousness" into the very fabric of your organizational culture. By cause consciousness I mean your organization meaningfully and systemically:

- Commits to being a pro-active, socially-focused, caring company

- Creates partnerships with other sectors and aids their mission in service to people or environmental issues in need

- Makes all business decisions based on doing good, not just on making money

- Engages all your stakeholders, internally and externally, in this cause consciousness culture

- Commits to a future where your organization's success is in direct relationship to the benefit you provide for others

When you do this, when you and all involved with your organization practice this cultural shift, people will take notice. Cause consciousness will affect your employees, and they will like working for your company. They will talk to others about the good things your company is doing and how they themselves are participating in these good efforts. And this will raise their morale and their job satisfaction, and they will stay longer with your company. Your customers and all business relations will notice this change and this will increase your sales, your brand recognition and your customer loyalty. You will start to favorably stand out against your competition. The media will be attracted to your company and provide press coverage on what you are doing to benefit your community. Your community will start talking about your organization, your people and your importance to the community. And because of all this, your organization will begin to grow, you will start to make more money... and you will begin to glow.

The Story of Glow

I grew up in northeastern Ohio where there are millions of fireflies. These wonderful little creatures come out when it's dark and usually when it's very warm. A firefly creates its own light, glowing from within.

In a similar way, people can also create that inner glow which can become visible to others. For inside all of us there is light. We say smart people are bright. Happy people have a sunny disposition. Don't we call the best among us stars? When someone falls in love or a woman becomes pregnant, we say they have a glow about them…because they do. It isn't a visible light. It's an energy that can be seen on their faces and felt in our hearts. And we are drawn to it.

It's no different with an organization. An organization is nothing more than a group of people. And when they're collectively focused on a higher purpose, when they have embedded a cause consciousness, when they've entered into meaningful collaboration with organizations in other sectors to create a greater good in society - that organization will glow. Everyone inside and all around such an organization will be warmed and attracted by that glow.

I use our firefly "Glow" as a guide throughout this book. When you see her, expect something glowingly important.

Glowing Companies

Throughout this book we will explore examples of cross-sector partnerships. I will always encourage you to find models to learn from - their successes, their challenges and their mistakes. What does a glowing company look like, what are those models? I'm sure you've heard of the very good work of TOMS Shoes, The Container Store, Build-A-Bear, Southwest Airlines, Life is Good and many more. These organizations have embedded a cause consciousness deep into the very DNA of their corporate culture. I am constantly on the lookout for organizations that are glowing. And so it is such a thrill when I witness the good works of Autodesk, Better World Books, Umpqua Bank, Bon Appétit Management Company, and more that may not have received the recognition they deserve but are glowing or on their way to being glowing companies.

I have put case studies of several of these companies in the **Resource Center** which I encourage you to read, and I suggest that you visit their websites and read their annual reports, particularly the sections on company philosophy, sustainability programs, community involvement and employee volunteer participation.

One example of a Glowing company is the outdoor apparel and equipment company Patagonia. Yvon Chouinard, Patagonia's founder, began rock climbing at the age of 14, and when he began his company, it focused on selling rock climbing equipment. As he branched out into clothing he did so with the philosophy of being in business to make a meaningful social change. And his was the first company to recycle fleece and the first company to use all organic cotton. Patagonia's goal is to "use business to inspire and implement solutions to the environmental crisis."

Patagonia produces high-quality environmentally friendly garments that command significant price premiums. Its environmental mission motivates it not only to donate to environmental causes and reduce the impact of its own production, but also to share its practices with other companies. Patagonia is able to maintain a larger gross profit margin than its competitors.

Patagonia has an Environmental Internship Program which provides that after one year of service, Patagonia employees may volunteer up to two months for an environmental non-profit of their choosing and earn their regular salary. They also have a program where employees may take Field Days to test their gear and get paid. And if these aren't cool enough, "Let My People Go Surfing" is Patagonia's flextime policy. Basically, you cannot schedule your surf time, you need to surf when the surf is good. So, Patagonia employees are trusted to get their job done and use the flextime to take advantage of the outdoors. This highly rare combination of service to the environment and enjoying the environment go hand-in-hand, naturally.

Patagonia, like other companies that seem to glow, has made giving back to society an integral part of its overall business plan. This is not just good corporate social responsibility - this is a sound business strategy. When Patagonia and other socially conscious, forward-thinking companies provide such benefits, especially paid time off for participating in doing good for society, they see the results come streaming back in – in employee loyalty, dramatically decreased employee turnover, increased productivity, better customer relationships, and a better bottom-line.

So is it any surprise that Patagonia receives 15,000 resumes each year for about 100 open positions? So they can pick the very best employees. It's a wonderful cycle. Treat your employees well, they'll stay with you and you'll attract the best.

Patagonia does very well while it is also focused on doing good. Patagonia glows.

Another glowing company is Better World Books. CEO, Andy Perlmutter, offered this quote:

"Better World Books is about collaborative consumption – we enable people to share their pre-loved books, rather than sending them to landfills. In the process they can raise much needed funding for literacy and education in support of local communities – and that is the essence of our business – doing well by doing good and supporting institutions that are the pillars of healthy communities in our world."

New Organizations Building a Foundation for Glowing

What is most exciting is the rapidly growing movement of combining good business and doing good by those starting new businesses. Across the globe, and certainly in the United States, the Millennial generation and others are starting businesses based on the cause consciousness philosophy. More and more, these startup organizations are on the track to becoming glowing companies.

Another very exciting trend, especially among baby boomers, is people retiring from their former business lives and starting nonprofit organizations, or providing their expertise to support existing nonprofits. The wealth of talent in this trend is simply extraordinary. Cross-sector partnerships should come naturally to those who are moving from one sector to another.

Case studies of several of these soon-to-be glowing businesses can be found in the **Resource Center**, but let me share one here.

I am working as an advisor to Clear Ear, a medical device startup company that spun out of Stanford University's Biodesign program in 2011. The two founders, Lily Truong and Dr. Vandana Jain, are all about wanting to do good for society, while they are developing a profitable company. So they reached out to me to assist in the development of their foundational social good philosophy, or what I call their cause consciousness. They have an established policy where they will donate their resources: 1% of people, 1% of product, and 1% of profits. Obviously, as a startup, in the first couple of years these donations won't be large. However, this foundational philosophy will serve their company, all involved and the greater good as they grow.

This policy may sound familiar to those of you that know Salesforce.com. Salesforce was founded on the same policy of donating 1% of their product, 1% of their revenue and 1% of their employees' time. And that policy has helped them become a leader in their field and grow to over $3 billion in annual sales. I first heard about Salesforce.com when they proactively came to us at the American Red Cross and offered 50 free licenses on their cloud-based CRM platform. Today they will give free software to any nonprofit that applies to the Salesforce Foundation.

Whether you are just starting a company or are part of a long-established organization, embedding a cause consciousness into your culture will provide multiple benefits, position your company for growth and success, and create a greater good for society. When you become a glowing company you take win-win to an entirely new level.

Now that you understand the ultimate goal - to become a glowing organization -we will begin laying the foundation for your transition. First we will review the basics of cross-sector partnerships and cause marketing and then undertake a step-by-step guided journey in the development of your own programs, projects or campaigns.

PART II

UNDERSTANDING CROSS-SECTOR PARTNERSHIPS AND CAUSE MARKETING

Each sector of nonprofit, for-profit, education or government has attributes, policies, missions and business practices which vary somewhat to significantly from those of the other sectors. In the development of cross-sector partnerships, this can be both a blessing and a challenge. Experience shows, however, that the benefits of cross-sector partnerships far outweigh whatever obstacles or challenges may arise.

For the past three years, our firm has issued *The Burtch Report*, a survey of primarily small to midsize nonprofit and for-profit organizations. Included in the survey is the question: "What misconceptions do you feel the for-profit community has about the nonprofit community?" And of the for-profit organizations, "What misconceptions do you feel the nonprofit community has about the for-profit community?" The results over the past three years show that in far too many cases nonprofits and for-profits don't understand each other's business models or philosophies, or how to work with each other effectively.

Challenges aside, these responses also speak the truth and thus provide pathways for better understanding and for the successful development of partnerships.

Here is a small sampling from *The Burtch Report*:

What Nonprofits Say About For-Profits

The biggest challenge is helping the for-profit understand the value of non-profits and how they can think outside the box to create a true partnership.

- For-profits have difficulty in understanding the full cost associated with delivery of nonprofit's obligation in partnerships.

- Making contact (and a connection) with the person(s) who has the ability to determine whether or not to support our organization in one form or another is often very challenging.

- Unrealistic expectations of results: their ROI (return on investment) expectations are too high.

- Short-changing necessary operating costs, such as insisting all funds go to program/ direct service, leaving no money for execution

- All they want to do is use my logo and reputation to sell more products.

- I don't trust that they really believe in our cause.

- We need their money, but we could lose our reputation.

- They're really not interested in helping us develop our services or grow our volunteer base.

- Different understandings of the value of our work; For-profits are trying to fit our work into their marketing objectives instead of looking at the partnership as equal parts nonprofit mission and for-profit marketing.

What For-Profits Say About Nonprofits

- They think their logo is worth far more than it really is in the marketplace.

- They move far too slowly to match our business style and aggressive marketing plans.

- Everything has to be decided by a committee. Where is the leadership there?

- They put up so many obstacles, especially saying that doing such and such could harm their reputation.

- Wouldn't it be easier to do something on our own than to complicate things by working with a nonprofit organization?

- Let's face it - the smartest people don't go work for nonprofits… there's no money in it.

- They just don't know how to run a business.

- They have a different culture and value sets.

- They lack clarity as to most important outcomes they are committed to achieving.

- Lack of resources, lack of innovation, minimal accountability

These quotes speak volumes about how far apart the relationship can be at the start. Yet these challenges can be overcome because your common goals and opportunities are great. It simply boils down to beginning with an open mind, developing clear communication and above all, being totally honest about your organization's objectives, needs and limitations

Karen Baker, California Secretary of Service and Volunteering, said "Some of the nuances in the private and nonprofit sector can make (partnerships) challenging. For example, it is tough for nonprofits to understand the private sector – their interests, their challenges, and their language. The same is true of the private sector fully understanding the nonprofit world. In order to have mutually beneficial partnerships, it is critical to have an honest understanding of what each party is seeking out of the relationship. Open dialogue and communication at the onset of a partnership is so critical, and often times, that is what is missing."

While there may be some operational and philosophical differences between the sectors, be especially careful not to assume the individuals within a certain sector operate or think alike. Like you and me, everyone is different. Your predisposition as to how a particular sector operates could become a major obstacle in any constructive cross-sector communication or partnership.

In *Getting to Yes, Negotiating Agreement Without Giving In*, Roger Fisher and William Ury emphasize that while it is important to "pay attention to differences of belief and custom, avoid stereotyping individuals. Different groups and places have different customs and beliefs. Know and respect them but be aware about making assumptions about individuals." Such assumptions based on their group characteristics are "insulting, as well as risky. It denies that person his or her individuality."

In developing cross-sector partnerships, you are not really working with different sectors as much as working with individual people from these sectors. That is where the focus of open and honest communication must lie. All sectors - nonprofit, for-profit, education and government - have different cultures, different business practices, different histories and different approaches. These differences are what make cross-sector partnerships so exciting and so successful. Just don't shoot yourself in the foot by presuming that you understand the other sectors, because until you've walked a mile in their shoes...you really don't. Let's explore a cross-sector partnership that was extremely successful, though it had significant challenges of misunderstanding and miscommunications to overcome, some of which were never completely resolved.

Against All Odds:
Tenderloin After-School Program

Leadership San Francisco is a year-long program sponsored by the San Francisco Chamber of Commerce that promotes civic engagement, made up of participants from the nonprofit, for-profit, education and government sectors. Our forty-member class spent a day experiencing the crime-ridden San Francisco district known as The Tenderloin.

Besides the proliferation of adult bookstores, strip clubs, bars and a significant amount of homeless people milling around the filthy streets, what struck us was the number of young children we saw using these streets, sidewalks and storefronts as their playground.

Motivated to do something, a couple members of our class met with San Francisco School Superintendent Ramon Cortines. He advised that "the most pressing need for these inner-city children was a safe, quiet, creative place to go after school." We then ap-

Photo courtesy of Nita Winter

proached Brother Kelly Cullen, Executive Director of the Tenderloin Neighborhood Development Corporation (TNDC), a non-profit provider of low income housing, which owned a building on Eddy Street, dead center in The Tenderloin. Leasing a portion of the first floor of this building was Connie's Bar, a seedy, prostitute-laden establishment with the sign posted prominently on the front door "No one under 21 allowed."

I proposed to our class that we take over Connie's Bar and turn it into a free educational, recreational and cultural center for the children of The Tenderloin. It was an idea so large and so ripe with challenge that it took nearly 5 meetings for our class to agree that we just had to do this. As the loudest proponent of this outrageous idea, I was chosen to spearhead the endeavor.

First we formed a partnership between Leadership San Francisco and TNDC. Seeking a prominent leader of the San Francisco business community, we enticed Holger Gantz, general manager of the Hilton Hotel and Towers, which bordered upon The Tenderloin to join our partnership. Holger enthusiastically led the fundraising drive which attracted Pacific Telesis, Koret Foundation, Gap, Bank of America, Wells Fargo Bank, PG&E and many others. Additional members of the hospitality and construction industries and members of the general community rushed to join the effort. Together we did what no one thought was possible - in one year we raised over $200,000, secured the lease on Connie's Bar, completely renovated the space, built a small children's library, computer room, director's office and play room. On July 13, 1993 the Tenderloin After-School Program opened.

Along the way, an astonishing level of media coverage and diverse public support was received - all on a volunteer basis. An editorial in the *San Francisco Examiner* summed it up nicely: "In the real world... progress, if any, is measured inch by inch through gauntlets of frustration, bureaucracy, broken promises and, of course, lack of money. So let's congratulate the enthusiastic people of Leadership San Francisco '92...and all who made this dream come true."

President Bill Clinton, Senator Dianne Feinstein, San Francisco Mayor Frank Jordan and many others wrote letters of commendation. President Clinton wrote, "These kinds of bold initiatives require a partnership between business community resources and local non-profit experience."

And today, rather than using peep show signs as their jungle gym, the children of The Tenderloin have a clean, safe place to go after school. That's the very great news.

Perhaps the biggest challenge for this project was bringing together a highly diverse partnership team. The Tenderloin Neighborhood Development Corporation owned the building that housed Connie's Bar but was unable to provide further financial support. The Leadership San Francisco class of 1992 was a small volunteer group of young men and women who could work hard but who also lacked the financial wherewithal to undertake such a costly project. The low-income community surrounding the proposed after-school program strongly favored the opportunity to provide a safe, off-the-streets place for their children, but could not financially support the project.

Most surprising was the resistance from one of the Tenderloin Neighborhood Development Corporation's own program managers, whose programs would most directly benefit from the new after-school program. This program manager created an an-

Photo courtesy of Tenderloin After-School Program

tagonistic relationship with the Leadership San Francisco volunteers and made it clear, in no uncertain terms, that we were coming in from the "outside" to push our way into her area of responsibility. Whether this reaction was due to cultural differences, turf resistance or other misunderstanding factors, her defiance flew in the face of everything this project stood for - helping the children. Obviously, the after-school program could not have been accomplished without the significant "outside" help we brought to bear.

I have never fully comprehended this defiance and I use it as a teaching moment for myself in the development of cross-sector partnerships. Striving to understand personal agendas and misconceptions, especially those that can potentially sabotage a project focused on doing good, is a valuable exercise in your partnership development process.

Sadly, for nearly 20 years, nowhere in the promotional literature or website of the Tenderloin Neighborhood Development Corporation, which houses and manages the after-school program, was there any mention of this unique partnership, or all of the community businesses, organizations and volunteers who worked so hard to create and fund the program. And no acknowledgment was given to the Leadership San Francisco team that inspired and drove its existence. Indeed, their website stated: "The Tenderloin After-School Program (TASP) was started with the help of parents in one of TNDC's buildings." That's it, and it was simply not the truth. TNDC took all the donated help and in spite of the mountain of evidence to the contrary, took all the credit, too.

Note: As I was editing the final version of this book, I received an invitation from the Tenderloin Neighborhood Development Corporation to attend the 20th Anniversary celebration of the opening of the Tenderloin After-School program. I had mixed reactions to this invitation. On the one hand, I was so proud of our class and all the other community partners involved for our accomplishment which has served thousands of vulnerable inner-city children during the past 20 years. But on the other hand, I was still upset about the untruth that had been told for so long. I decided to try one more time and wrote the Executive Director of TNDC asking him to give credit to our Leadership Class of 1992 and the many other people and organizations who had contributed so much. I accompanied this request with the quotes from President Bill Clinton, Senator Dianne Feinstein and other notables praising "the partnership." To my very pleasant surprise, he responded favorably and by the event on May 17, 2013, the TNDC website gave the long overdue credit, as did the Executive Director from the podium at the celebration event.

The challenges of the Tenderloin After-School Program point out that there are often distinct differences between the business practices, philosophy and personalities of each person and each sector. Indeed, organizations and individuals coming together will have personal agendas that they bring to the partnership. As we just saw, these personal agendas can sometimes be quite negative, however, in most cases, addressing and respecting individual agendas and objectives can be quite positive for the partnership.

Welcoming Individual Agendas

In almost every case, each partner will have specific reasons and business objectives for why he/she wants to explore a partnership. These individual "agenda items" are important. For example, for-profit organizations are usually looking to increase the sales of their products or services or expand their community goodwill. They may want an opportunity for their employees to engage as volunteers on community projects which will expand their knowledge, skills and job satisfaction. Nonprofit organizations are usually seeking funding, sponsorship of their events, volunteers, in-kind donations of equipment, technical expertise or other needs.

In many cases, these initial agenda items are just the proverbial tip of the iceberg. When you drill into the many benefits, opportunities or linkages that can be developed, between the different sectors in a partnership, the list will become extensive.

You should openly share all your important agenda items with your potential partners. In fact, I strongly encourage you to put all your cards face up on the table and discuss freely what you are seeking from the potential partner relationship. And I recommend that you do so at your very first meeting. When your potential partner understands your specific marketing and organizational objectives, they are in a much better position to work with you to meet them. And when they share their specific marketing and organizational objectives, you will be far more open and motivated to help meet their objectives. This open approach to partnership is the beginning of a trusting relationship, and as with any relationship, successful cross-sector partnerships begin and end with trust.

Laura Pincus Hartman is Director, External Partnerships for Zynga, the hugely successful online game company. When asked how she is able to get nonprofit and for-profit organizations to stop hiding their agendas and start working collaboratively together, she commented: "I think the purpose is not to get them to shed their agendas, but it certainly is to encourage them to shed misconceptions and to break through existing mental models and preconceived notions. However, in fact, you want every partner to bring with them their agendas, their vested interests, because it's those interests that are going to serve to motivate them. So, you're not asking for-profits to leave profit interests at the door, or leave all of your interests at the door, because it's that profit motive that motivates, that encourages, and that's going to influence them to make the best possible decisions. You want each stakeholder to do what it does best and then we also need, of course, our nonprofit partners. You want those nonprofit partners to do what they do best."

By presenting all of your agenda items in a partnership you're not being selfish or trying to overreach in your expectations. You are simply asking the question: What if? And it's a very important question to ask. If we develop a strong, trusting, lasting relationship, could we potentially receive all or most of our organization's objectives? And what could we potentially give back to our partner? Motivating and helping each other meet or preferably exceed individual objectives and thus create the much desired win-win approach - is the primary goal of cross-sector partnerships, along with creating a greater good through your partnership.

Turning the Tables: Presenting a Business Value Proposition

The usual nonprofit/for-profit scenario is that the for-profit organization is providing funding in a more philanthropic manner, while the nonprofit is seeking funding to meet the needs of its organization's mission and services to the community. Business value is rarely part of the equation. Yet providing a mutually beneficial business value is what creates a strong attractiveness to work together and subsequently, a much more lasting bond between the organizations.

Think about the typical situation. A nonprofit organization has a particular need or program it wishes to develop that requires external funding. They write up a carefully prepared description of this need, how many people it will impact and how this need or program will further their community mission. They certainly will estimate the amount of money that seems reasonable to request from a corporate funder. This amount may be based on the for-profit's past giving history to this organization, or what the for-profit has given to other nonprofits before. The nonprofit is very careful not to ask for too much, yet they want to ask for enough to impact their need.

The nonprofit also realizes that the corporate funder or local business is probably being approached by many other nonprofit organizations seeking funding. So they want their presentation to have dramatic impact, a strong case for funding. That is usually the nonprofit's primary focus - a strong argument for the needs of their cause.

Now let's turn the tables and look at this situation from the for-profit organization's point of view. Imagine you are a for-profit executive who has been listening to or reading proposals like these typical nonprofit pitches, over and over again. And in walks a nonprofit executive with a well thought out, business value proposition which clearly shows that by working with their nonprofit your for-profit business will receive multiple benefits - benefits such as increased sales of your products or services, ways to increase the morale of your employees, opportunities that will raise your brand awareness, and a long list of other benefits. Now that is a very different approach. Which would be most effective?

What I mean by business value proposition is that each side addresses the marketing and business objectives of the potential partner. They have done their homework, read the other organization's promotional materials and annual report, conducted an Internet search for press coverage and other information about their potential partner, maybe even talked to a friend who works or volunteers at that organization, and so they have a good understanding of the business priorities of this potential partner. With this understanding, they put together a presentation which shows that by working with their organization (for-profit, nonprofit, education or government), multiple benefits towards the other's business or mission objectives can be achieved through a partnership.

This is the business value proposition approach, and it is by far the most successful way to create a lasting cross-sector partnership and bring multiple benefits to all partners. By understanding this business value mindset you have a huge advantage over your competition, no matter which sector or side of the partnership equation you come from.

A case in point: Two friends of mine, Sheila Jones and Kathy Eggert, are Northern California artists who founded a program called Art from the Heart. They bring local artists, musicians, dancers and other creative artists into schools where, unfortunately, there are little to no creatively expressive opportunities. I have a particular empathy for one of these challenged schools, San Pedro Elementary School in San Rafael, CA, as my stepdaughter was a second grade teacher there. Nearly 100% of San Pedro students are His-

Art from the Heart mural at San Pedro Elementary School

panic children, almost all of whom are bused to the school. For most of these children, English is their second language, and a large percentage of their parents speak no English at all. Because the school receives no budget for the arts and the children's parents are, for the most part, unable to provide financial support, San Pedro was void of artistic programs, other than a play put on each year by the teachers and one violin program that reaches about six children. This school met all the criteria for an Art from the Heart program, but had no available funding.

Sheila, Kathy and I were talking one day about corporate funding and I asked what their budget was for the year. They said it was a little over $9,000 for supplies and the small stipend they give to their guest artists. I asked them if they had ever thought about going to Autodesk, which is headquartered in San Rafael, almost right down the road, and forming a partnership with them. Autodesk is a multi-billion dollar, multinational computer design company full of artists and designers and other highly creative people. They said they couldn't imagine that a company as big as Autodesk would be interested in their very small program.

I was able to set up a meeting between Sheila and Kathy and the Autodesk Grants Committee (SF Bay Area). After making a few introductory remarks, I sat back and let Sheila and Kathy run the show. They began by saying how at first they hesitated to contact Autodesk. But after reading their community relations guidelines and other information that was publicly available, they felt that they could bring them an opportunity that would be of significant benefit for Autodesk.

They explained how Autodesk employees could get involved with Art from the Heart, how fun and valuable it would be to the employees and how this program would provide highly favorable publicity and goodwill all over the community because of Autodesk employees working with these low income children in these challenging schools.

During the meeting they poured out their hearts about the needs of these children, and how artistic expression was so important for children's personal growth and educational success. They showed pictures of the children making murals, gluing seashells around picture frames and other art projects. Their presentation was heartfelt and convincing.

The five members of the Autodesk Grants Committee were totally engaged. As a matter of fact, one member was a cellist in the Golden Gate Orchestra, two were graphic designers, and one was a puppeteer. Every one of them wanted to volunteer with Art from the Heart. The meeting ended with hugs and hearty handshakes.

A few weeks later, Art from the Heart received a $5,000 donation - over half of its annual budget. Most surprisingly, this $5,000 was up to ten times the amount Autodesk normally gives to a first-time grantee. Autodesk would even pay for the time spent by their volunteers working on the program. Their generous donation would not only bring artistic programs to San Pedro Elementary School, but also help to expand their programs to other schools within the San Rafael School District which met the same criteria.

Kathy and Sheila had presented Autodesk with an opportunity to get involved with children at risk, in their schools, in a very creative and meaningful way.

The key lesson from the Autodesk/Art from the Heart relationship is that while they were immensely different in size and organizational focus, they had the advantage of providing a business value proposition to each other. In the case of Autodesk, they were able to provide funding, volunteers, and lend significant credibility to a small organization through this relationship. Undoubtedly, Art from the Heart will emphasize their relationship with Autodesk in future funding and partnership requests, which should increase their attractiveness to other for-profit organizations. Art from the Heart provided a business value proposition to Autodesk in the form of employee engagement, good community relations and helping to address Autodesk's Corporate Social Responsibility objectives.

I have worked with well over 100 nonprofits and rarely have I seen nonprofits utilize this business value proposition approach. Yet this is exactly how for-profit businesses operate internally. A corporate marketing or sales proposal will not see the light of day unless it provides a solid business value proposition for increasing their business. In other words: If it doesn't make dollars, it doesn't make sense.

So it cuts both ways. If you don't take the effort to understand the needs and business objectives of your potential partner, how can you possibly expect them to want to support and engage in the needs and business objectives of your organization? Of course the good news is, when you present a solid business value proposition and carefully listen to theirs, you have the foundation for a truly successful cross-sector partnership.

Creating Multiple Links Between Organizations

While funding was certainly an important aspect of the Art from the Heart and Autodesk partnership, what convinced these two organizations to work together was how each would bring multiple benefits to the other. For example, when the employees of Autodesk volunteer their creative talents to work in schools as part of the Art from the Heart programming, a bond or linkage is formed between the nonprofit organization, the sponsoring for-profit, and the students in the classrooms. Over time these linkages become very strong as the participants engage intellectually, physically and emotionally with the students, schools and each other. And these linkages will begin to expand, from the initial links of funding and then personal involvement, to the press coverage this effort may draw, the employee satisfaction that will be generated, the potential of putting an Autodesk employee on the Board of Directors of Art from the Heart, the community recognition and goodwill that will be stimulated, and so forth. As the partners enjoy these growing opportunities of working together and see the benefits come pouring out, their relationship and organizations will be linked strongly together on many levels.

Imagine two pieces of leather connected by one simple thread. You hold one piece and your friend holds the other. Now imagine that you both pull on the separate pieces of leather. The thread breaks very easily. Now imagine the two pieces of leather are connected by three threads. You pull again. You feel a brief bit of resistance from the three threads, but still they break without much effort. Now imagine that there are 10 threads connecting the two pieces of leather. Now pull, pull hard. With quite a bit of effort you might be able to break a few of the threads, but probably not all 10. In any case, the resistance was strong, the bond of the 10 threads held firmly.

And so it is with cross-sector partnerships. When the relationship consists of only one linkage between the organizations, let's say the for-profit organization buys tickets to a nonprofit's annual fundraising dinner, that link (or thread) can easily be broken. For example, no one from the for-profit organization may actually go to the dinner but it wanted to show their support for the nonprofit's mission. There was no bond, no real relationship. Now imagine that there are three links between the for-profit and the nonprofit – the for-profit organization bought the fundraising dinner tickets, had donated some used computer equipment to the nonprofit and some of their employees spent a Saturday painting the nonprofit's dining room where they provide free meals to the homeless. Now there is a pretty strong relationship with these three linkages between the organizations. Each year when the for-profit reviews their community relationships and contribution strategy, they will look favorably upon this nonprofit organization where they have developed three good links.

Now imagine the two organizations have developed 5, 6 maybe even up to 10 linkages. Now imagine trying to pull these two organizations apart. It's very difficult, indeed darn near impossible, to break apart such a strong, binding relationship.

I use this example for two reasons. When multiple linkages are developed between the for-profit and nonprofit organization, a very strong bond and relationship is established over the years. This non-profit organization is uppermost in the for-profit's contribution strategy. Their employees are volunteering time to serve that nonprofit and their organization is receiving the benefit of higher morale and employment retention because of the satisfaction they receive from working in the community on their company's behalf. Going down the list of potential linkages, the individual partners realize that many if not all of those involved in their organization have become engaged in this relationship, and all are benefiting from it. So much good is coming from this relationship, from these linkages and benefits.

The second reason I give this example is what happens in challenging economic times. When a down economy may cause a for-profit company to struggle, they will look to areas where they can decrease their expenses, and naturally, one of the areas they will analyze is their corporate philanthropy and their nonprofit relationships. If their management, community relations department or foundation decides to reduce their annual contributions by say 10%, who will they cut out of their nonprofit funding or partnership plan? Yes, the easiest to come off the list are those organizations where they have the fewest linkages. While these nonprofits may be doing good work in the community and the company likes supporting them, the bond between the nonprofit organizations and the company is rather weak.

Now just try to recommend pulling funding and company support away from the organization with whom the company has spent many years developing a close and strong partnership relationship, and where they have 5, 6, or maybe 10 linkages. One of the company's senior managers is probably sitting on the Board of Directors of that nonprofit organization, and they certainly are going to object. The company's employees who feel great pride in their commitment and volunteerism to that nonprofit will not want to see any change. The media coverage that the company has received from the relationship would stop and they don't want to see that happen. There is a long list of reasons why the for-profit will not want to sever ties with organizations where they have developed such strong linkages.

This is also a very clear message to nonprofit organizations. In difficult economic times, the companies that have the strongest linkages and partnerships with a nonprofit will, to the extent that they can, fight hard to continue to keep that partnership going. They have too much to lose and will receive too much resistance from their employees and all those involved with their organization. In most cases, they will look to lessen or possibly terminate their relationships/ funding with other nonprofit organizations with whom they have fewer linkages and a weaker relationship. Don't be on that list.

Nonprofit, for-profit, education or government sector - it doesn't matter. The more threads, the more benefits developed between the organizations through cross-sector partnerships, the stronger and more lasting the relationship becomes, and the benefits to all partners and their stakeholders continue to grow.

Multiple-Sector Partnerships

Some of the best cross-sector partnerships involve three, and sometimes all four, of the nonprofit, for-profit, education and government sectors. While it may seem more complicated, in many cases the more sectors you have involved in a partnership, the better. Each partner brings a different perspective to the partnership, different business objectives, valuable intelligence, new assets, volunteers, and much more. The biggest challenge is managing all of these people, assets and opportunities. It's what I call an "abundance management problem," and it's a very nice problem to have.

Fishing in the City

One of my favorite examples of a four-sector partnership is Fishing in the City, begun by the California Department of Fish and Game. This program has been in operation for many years, and it just keeps getting better. Fishing in the City focuses on creating sustainable programs that create repeatable experiences for children. It is not enough to take a kid fishing, they must learn how to do it on their own and have access to the equipment, materials, lakes, and fish near where they live or their parents work. A typical community partnership includes schools, service clubs, local park agencies, water districts, and businesses.

This program has three primary goals:

1) Teach kids and their families to fish

2) Improve fishing in urban areas (near home and work)

3) Help residents learn how individual actions affect the quality of water in local streams, creeks, and bays

These goals are accomplished through the creation of local partnerships that offer community-based programs. Potential partners include any organization, agency, or business interested in fish, fishing, kids, and/or clean water. Ethan Rotman who works for the California Department of Fish and Game has coordinated the San Francisco Bay Area program since 1995. The program is so successful, it is used as a model by other states and has been adopted by Rotary International for use across the country (They call it "Rotary Fish").

The largest and most successful program is "South Bay Fishing in the City" which serves youth and their families in the Santa Clara Valley of California. The many partners in this program include:

1) County of Santa Clara

2) City of San Jose

3) Bay Area Sport Fishers

4) California Department of Fish and Game

5) Rotary International

6) San Jose School District

7) Tackle Manufacturers and Retailers

8) US Fish and Wildlife

9) Boys and Girls Clubs

Working together, these organizations coordinate 15 learn-to-fish events annually in the Santa Clara Valley. Each event brings in additional local sponsors and partners. According to Rotman, "Part of the longevity of the program is the variety of partners. When one agency faces cutbacks, another partner is able to step forward and fill the gap. Over the years each partner has ebbed and flowed in and out with their ability to participate, but the program has never been in danger of collapse."

I particularly like this partnership because not only are all four sectors involved (nonprofit, for-profit, education and government) but like the Levi's/Special Olympics soccer ball story earlier, there are many linkages involved with Fishing in the City: volunteerism, education, in-kind donations, in-school activities, adults working with children, community involvement, corporate funding, media relationships and more. The strength and power of this innovative cross-sector partnership program is because of these multiple linkages.

This multi-sector, multi-linkage approach worked wonderfully in a partnership to bring much-needed health and wellness services to a very low income population in Oakland, California.

5th Annual Health and Wellness Fair

Ramsell Corporation provides services to agencies that serve underserved populations. It also owns The Apothecary in Eastmont Town Center, a shopping mall in the low-income and predominantly African-American area of East Oakland.

"The Apothecary is a community pharmacy inside of Eastmont and has been in business for almost 50 years," stated Eric Flowers, CEO of Ramsell. "We have held 4 Health Fairs in the past. This year we wanted to attract a far larger audience to take advantage of all the free health services, but to do so we needed to find partners." They asked for my help and I had the honor of co-directing a rather extraordinary four-sector partnership for the 5th Annual Health and Wellness Fair.

Our first partner was the office of California State Assemblymember Sandré R. Swanson, which had held a Health Fair in the past, but for staff and budget limitations, had decided not to continue their event for 2012. In reviewing our separate agendas, we realized that this was an excellent match. Assemblymember Swanson was deeply committed to bettering the lives of his low-income constituents. Ramsell and The Apothecary wanted to provide a meaningful public service, especially in their home community of the East Bay, and more particularly, for the low income neighborhoods The Apothecary has been serving for nearly 50 years.

The Alameda County Public Health Department had also held a Health Fair in the past, and for similar reasons as the Assemblymember's office, had decided to discontinue their event for 2012. This government agency which provides multiple services to low income and underinsured populations was eager to join forces. To complete the lead partnership team, the Centers for Elders' Independence came on board. This nonprofit organization provides care for seniors age 55 and older with health problems that make it impossible for them to stay at home without the help of caregivers. Joining together, these four partners set out to do what none of them could have accomplished on their own.

As the planning for the greatly expanded Health Fair began to take shape, we reached out to Oakland Mayor Jean Quan and Nate Miley, President of the Board of Supervisors for Alameda County, to seek their personal and promotional support, which we received. Much needed and appreciated addi-

Photo by Bruce Burtch

tional financial support came from Kaiser Permanente and One Pacific Coast Bank. KTVU 2, the Fox TV affiliate for the San Francisco Bay Area, KBLX radio and Bay Area News Group, the largest newspaper group in the San Francisco Bay Area, joined in as the official media sponsors.

Ultimately, 90 health and wellness educational and professional organizations were attracted to this Health Fair, and they provided free services, such as dental, vision, blood pressure, HIV/AIDS testing, child immunizations, senior health, smoking cessation, asthma, and much more. At the end of the Health Fair, September 15, 2012, over 600 low income East Bay residents had received multiple free services from this amazing assembly of partners and health and wellness providers.

Photo by Bruce Burtch

The fitting climax to this extraordinary event was when a homeless woman, Brende White, who had pushed a shopping cart of all her belongings into the Health Fair, won a custom-made walker. She was delighted, the audience cheered boisterously, and our partnership team simply cried with happiness.

"This unique partnership is a perfect example of what can happen when concerned community-focused organizations see a common goal," commented Assemblymember Swanson later. "Combining the abilities of these diverse for-profit, nonprofit and governmental organizations means that far more Oakland and East Bay residents will benefit from the services provided at the Health Fair. This innovative partnership stands as a promising model for others to follow."

Angela Ball, Director, Public Health Nursing for the Alameda County Public Health Department said, "Though the Health Fair was just one day, it will have a lasting effect on underserved and underinsured residents, as it will link them to services they need for a better, healthier life."

Photo by Bruce Burtch

Yes, this was an extraordinary gathering of partners and providers, but it all grew from the simple idea that together we can do more than each of us on our own. And we all worked together with a shared mission and vision.

In the end, the overall cost of the Health Fair, including event management personnel, marketing and media materials, tables, chairs, signage, PA system, staging and security, was approximately $45,000. These costs were shared among the many partners and sponsors. The Bay Area media coverage value alone was probably five times this amount. Serving over 600 low-income residents in need of such health and wellness services, and the goodwill generated in the greater community for all partners and providers...priceless.

I can't tell you how many times I have been told by organizations in all sectors that they were challenged by finding good partnerships. My response is always the same, good partners are all around you, you just need to take the time to find them.

Win-Win: The Many Benefits of Cross-Sector Partnerships

To best appreciate the successes of cross-sector partnerships, stories are certainly helpful, but we also need to dig into the organizations themselves to understand how they tick and how they can work better with one or more partners.

From my experience, most people and the organizations they represent begin their exploration of a partnership with a fairly limited list of partnership goals. Usually the "ask" is fairly simple and straight-forward. The nonprofit might approach a for-profit organization for a donation to a particular project or program, or to sponsor a table at their annual fundraising gala. The for-profit organization may be seeking to raise the morale of its employees by arranging a one-day event where the employees would volunteer at a local homeless dining room or shelter. The misconception here is that cross-sector partnerships are not about philanthropy, cash donations, "one day and done" volunteer events, or sponsorships such as a breast cancer 3-day event or pledge walk. By definition, a partnership is a relationship. Many times there are contractual stipulations, but in nearly all cases, the partnership is based on a relationship meant to be long-term, jointly beneficial with many linkages.

In my workshops, participants are asked to write down all the benefits they think a nonprofit organization can receive by working with a for-profit organization in a partnership. Then we flip the exercise around, and they write down all the benefits they think a for-profit organization can receive by working in partnership with a nonprofit organization. And what I have found is startling.

To the question of how many distinct benefits a nonprofit can receive from partnering with a for-profit organization, the answer is, at least as of this writing: 31 distinct benefits. And to the question of how many benefits a for-profit organization can receive in a partnership with a nonprofit organization: 38 distinct benefits. That is one heck of a lot of benefits for each partner to receive in a partnership. However, what surprises my workshop attendees the most is the fact that for-profit organizations can potentially receive more benefit than can nonprofits. Most people think it would be the other way around.

These benefits are the real "secret sauce" of my work. There is an extraordinary amount of benefit that can be achieved by all partners in a well-designed, trusting, objectives- driven, cross-sector partnership. This has been proven so often over the last 35 years that I can make the following statement with absolutely no reservations:

There is nothing in business today that provides as much economic and social benefit, on as many levels, to as many stakeholders, as a strategic partnership between any combination of the nonprofit, for-profit, education and government sectors when focused on the greater good. Nothing else comes even close.

An innovative public relations program, the most clever social media campaign, the funniest or most emotional advertisement, the deepest discount or the biggest sale, the largest benefit race or the most successful fundraising gala - none of these can come even close to the multiple benefits that come from a cross-sector partnership.

Rather than detail all 31 nonprofit benefits and the 38 for-profit benefits here, I'm going to list the 10 most important ones, at least in my opinion, from each category. The complete listing of all 69 benefits can be found in the online **Resource Center**. By the way, you may be able to add even more benefits for either list, and I ask you to email me personally with your discoveries.

Benefits For-Profits Receive From Partnering With a Nonprofit Organization

Top 10 Benefits (These are not in any particular order, other than increasing sales, which is nearly always noted as number one.)

1) Increase sales of products or services

2) Increase employee engagement, job satisfaction and reduce turnover

3) Increase customer and brand loyalty

4) Attract the best employees through community involvement

5) Increase community goodwill by having your leadership and organization recognized for the good they create in society

6) Increase shareholder return

7) Reach new markets and new customer demographics

8) Increase employee skill development, teambuilding and leadership skills

9) Draw media attention and coverage for free

10) Attract new business partners and relationships

Key For-Profit Benefits

While each of these 10 top benefits is very important, I've chosen seven for closer examination:

Increase Sales of Products or Services

Cross-sector partnerships provide the rare opportunity of generating goodwill and helping those in need while also stimulating sales of your products and services.

In our earlier example of the Health and Wellness Fair, the primary objective of Ramsell Corporation as the lead partner was to be a good community citizen. This event also provided strong recognition and involvement of The Apothecary, the drugstore owned by Ramsell, which is located in the shopping center where the event was held. Thus the event's promotion would also drive business, over time, to The Apothecary.

Increase Employee Engagement, Job Satisfaction and Reduce Turnover

Extensive research has shown that when employees are allowed to engage in their community under the sponsorship of their employers, the morale of the employees increases significantly. The 2010 *Cone Cause Evolution Study* surveyed employees involved in their company's cause programs and found:

- 77% agreed with the statement: It's important for my company to provide employees with opportunities to become involved in causes.

- 79% agreed with the statement: I feel a strong sense of loyalty to my company.

- 57% agreed with the statement: My company's commitment to addressing social/environmental issues is one of the reasons I chose to work there.

AAA Northern California, Nevada & Utah won the National Award of Excellence from Points of Light Foundation for their employee volunteer programs. AAA provides up to 24 hours of paid time off for volunteering for company-supported community outreach initiatives through the AAA Volunteers program. Roger Hancock, Manager of Community Affairs, said: "By volunteering, employees are learning new skills, demonstrating and living AAA corporate values, improving AAA's reputation in the community, collaborating better with other divisions and departments, improving morale and deepening employee engagement, and having fun."

Richard Steckel and Robin Simons' book *Doing Best by Doing Good* published a study of 188 companies which found employee morale to be three times higher in firms heavily involved in their communities.

When morale is high, so is employee retention and that has a direct effect on the bottom-line of any organization. Employee turnover is expensive. A study by Bliss & Associates Inc. stated:

"It should be noted that the costs of time and lost productivity are no less important or real than the costs associated with paying cash to vendors for services such as advertising or temporary staff. These are all very real costs to the employer. These calculations will easily reach 150% of the employee's annual compensation figure. The cost will be significantly higher (200% to 250% of annual compensation) for managerial and sales positions."

It doesn't take a math whiz to figure out that when employee morale is high, they tend not to leave their companies, which lessens the organization's turnover rate, which reduces the significant cost of such turnover, and thus increases a company's profitability. Nice equation!

Increase Customer and Brand Loyalty

It would seem that nearly every company that sells a product or ser-

vice offers consumers some sort of a customer loyalty reward program - frequent flyer miles, credit card purchase rebates, buy 10 cups
of coffee and get your 11th free, the same deal at my local carwash,
upgrades to special concierge services at hotels and upscale specialty
retail stores, the list goes on and on. According to Colloquy research,
despite the recent recession, "U.S. consumer participation in rewards
programs is on the rise across all demographic segments...Consumers
are leaning on loyalty programs to stretch household budgets further
by earning rewards for their purchases."

From the business perspective, here are three good reasons why customer loyalty programs are so strong:

1) By encouraging customers to remain loyal, it helps to reduce a
   company's advertising and marketing budget.

2) It is easier and costs less (estimates are seven times less) to
   retain an existing customer than to attract a new customer.

3) When you know a customer's buying habits (think Costco) you
   can direct promotional programs to their specific areas of
   purchase interest.

A refreshing new trend has been added to this customer loyalty reward approach. By developing a relationship between your for-profit
company and a respected nonprofit where the nonprofit can raise funds
to support its mission, there has been a very positive response from
consumers. This sales and marketing oriented cross-sector partnership
approach is commonly known as cause marketing. Later on we will
explore cause marketing in detail. Studies by Cone, Inc. reinforce the
importance of cause marketing on increasing customer loyalty.

- 92% of the public has a more positive image of a company
  that supports a cause they care about.

- 85% of the general public and 92% of Moms want to buy a
  product that supports a cause.

- 87% of the general public and 93% of Moms are likely to
  switch from one product or service to another (price and quality

being equal) if the other product or service is associated with a good cause.

- 50% of the general public would try a new brand or one they've never heard of, if connected to a cause.

These are, obviously, incredible numbers. And they speak volumes on the importance of developing cause-related, cross-sector partnerships for your business. If you are the corporate marketing and sales director or a nonprofit development director reading this book, you should stop right here, put those statistics in a frame and mount them prominently on your wall. What other form of business/marketing can significantly raise your sales (or donations), lower your costs and build the retention and loyalty of your customers while generating community goodwill and supporting the mission of the nonprofit?

Attract the Best Employees Through Community Involvement

Every organization is looking to find the best employees and as we've all experienced, sometimes the employment application and resume don't tell the whole story. Andy Ball, former CEO of Webcor Builders, one of the nation's premier construction companies, found that Webcor's employee volunteerism and engagement in their community has been a tremendous benefit in attracting high caliber employees. According to Andy, "It started as a desire by a small group of individuals and it has become who we are. It defines how we act and defines the kind of people that are attracted to us and we, in turn, find that those are the best people to do the work. They perform the best, they are great people, they care, they are responsible and they take the leadership roles."

James Austin in *The Collaboration Challenge* noted "Conference Board survey of 454 companies revealed that 90% of managers believe that their company's community volunteer programs help these companies attract better employees. Company support for community service activities also enhances employee motivation and morale, thereby strengthening company loyalty and retention."

The *2009 PRWeek/Barkley PR Cause Survey* offered this quote from Chris Mann, Associate Integrated Marketing Manager for New Balance, regarding their company's 20-year association with Susan G. Komen for the Cure: "HR would tell you that it's big for recruitment and retention. It's been brought up in people's interviews as one of the reasons they respect the company." Mann said it was one of the things that attracted him to New Balance.

When you engage with your community and especially when you embed a cause consciousness into your organization, you will attract the best employees and this provides a definite competitive advantage.

Reach New Markets and
New Customer Demographics

According to Wikipedia, the term market share refers to "the percentage of a market (defined in terms of either units or revenue) accounted for by a specific entity." Marketers are keenly aware of the importance of developing as broad a market share as possible to support and preferably, increase their business. Two of the fastest growing demographics/market share opportunities for potential customers are the Generation Y/Millennials and seniors.

Generation Y

Gen Y, also known as Millennials, refers to people born in the 1980s and early 1990s. This generation is or should be of particular interest to marketers, as they have a very strong affinity to causes. The *2010 Cone Cause Evolution Study* stated that "college-aged Millennials have nearly $40 billion in discretionary income to spend. Still, each wants to shop wisely, and more than any other demographic group we tested, they buy with an eye toward the greater good." They buy... for the greater good!

This study also found that "Ninety-four percent of respondents ages 18-24 find it acceptable for a company to involve a cause or issue in its marketing (versus 88% average) and "they are much more willing to try new products because of a cause affiliation." The study also found that "Millennials' passion for supporting causes presents significant growth opportunities for companies as these young adults' income and purchasing power grows."

The study also suggests that "Millennials are the most socially-conscious consumers to date. In the past year, 81% of respondents have volunteered in some way (either weekly, monthly or once or twice a year). And 87% consider a company's cause commitments when deciding where to work."

Seniors

As a "Baby Boomer" myself, I find it increasingly difficult and somewhat embarrassing to admit that I qualify for the Senior Meal pricing at Denny's. The U.S. Census Bureau defines the Baby Boomers as those born between January 1st, 1946 and December 31st, 1964 and they make up about one-fourth of the U.S. population, or an estimated 78 million people. That's an enormous wave of people hitting or nearing retirement. Yet due to many financial factors, especially the recession of 2008-on, a large percentage of Baby Boomers plan to keep working. According to a recent AARP survey of Baby Boomers, 40% of them plan to work "until they drop."

Like the Millennials near the other end of the work age-spectrum, cross-sector partnerships offer an exceptional opportunity to expand your business into this vast marketplace of new "seniors" and of course, the 40.3 million other people 65 and older, according to the 2010 census.

Increase Employee Skill Development, Teambuilding and Leadership Skills

For many, the presumption is that the nonprofit organization benefits most when a business volunteer offers his or her services. Yet nothing could be further from the real truth. Ask anyone who has ever volunteered and they will probably tell you that they received as much, if not far more, from their volunteer experience than they gave. The obvious example for me is American Red Cross volunteers. They start their Red Cross training by learning CPR, emergency preparedness and other lifesaving skills. So right away they learn skills that could be of critical help in a life-threatening situation. When you see Red Cross workers at a disaster relief operation or a crisis communications center, you find people holding extremely responsible positions of leadership. They will be setting up and serving a shelter full of people displaced by the disaster, managing food delivery to the emergency shelter, directing communications and media relations, all the way up to the senior-most leadership positions where they are managing hundreds and possibly thousands of volunteers in a comprehensive disaster relief operation.

During the aftermath of the Hurricane Katrina disaster, a Red Cross volunteer (who worked for a trucking company) was tasked with the awesome responsibility of coordinating the transportation of food and supplies from all around the country to Louisiana. What type of employee was this woman, emblematic of all who serve in such trying situations, when she returned to her full-time job? Needless to say, she brought back a deep compassion for her fellow human beings and the extraordinary confidence that she could take on such a major assignment and handle it to near perfection. She came back with newfound and proven leadership abilities, and much more. She brought back with her new skills, new understanding and a deeper commitment than she may have ever had in her "real" job. She came back a much more valuable employee, a team-builder, and a leader.

Bobbi Silten, Chief Foundation Officer of Gap Foundation told me of Gap's proactive effort to place mid-level and entry-level Gap store personnel in community volunteer roles. These employees learned leadership and presentation skills, learned the ability to coordinate groups of people, to teach classes, and many other valuable lessons that would serve them well when they returned to their Gap store. And importantly, these were experiences and learning lessons that, for the most part, would not have been learned at that stage in their store employment.

A study by the National Survey of Giving, Volunteering and Participating found:

- 79% of volunteers said that their volunteer activities helped them with their interpersonal skills, such as understanding people better, motivating others, and dealing with difficult situations.

- 68% of volunteers said that volunteering helped them to develop better communication skills.

- 63% reported increased knowledge about issues related to their volunteering.

- 23% said they volunteered to acquire job-related skills and improve job opportunities.

Nonprofits need volunteers, for in many cases they are the lifeblood of their organization. Volunteering is, most definitely, a two-way street. It's just that sometimes a lot more traffic is heading back to the for-profit employer.

Draw Media Attention and Coverage for Free

Every organization, from every sector, wants to attract favorable coverage from the media. In many cases, getting such free publicity is challenging for a for-profit business. In some industries, such as oil, tobacco, alcoholic beverages and gambling, garnering favorable free publicity is quite rare, even when they are doing good work for their communities.

When I became the national writer for cross-sector partnerships and cause marketing for Examiner.com, I began a series called Profiles in Partnership. To date I have interviewed over 25 senior executives from the for-profit, nonprofit, education and government sectors in order to share their advice and experiences in cross-sector partnerships. Many of the quotes throughout this book are taken from these one-on-one interviews. In one interview with the oil giant Chevron I was told they were quite surprised that I was there to interview them about their cause-related work. One executive said that they almost didn't grant the interview because they were "pretty sure it was going to be negative." That has been their conditioning in working with the media.

I cite this story because that is the general climate in today's media/ business relationship - one of skepticism and distrust, as we clearly saw in our discussion on misconceptions. So here's the good news: even skeptics in the media and others can be won over when they see your organization is forming an honest and valuable partnership with a nonprofit organization to help the underserved in your community.

Chevron and its Richmond, California refinery formed a partnership with Catholic Charities of the East Bay and together developed a program called Project B-Mat, which stands for Bilingual Medical Assistant Training. This partnership was developed to support and train low income, limited-English speaking residents to secure employment as clinical medical assistants in high-demand occupations in the East Bay of the San Francisco Bay Area. To date, the program has enrolled more than 52 individuals, of which 37 have completed their externship at 16 different healthcare facilities, and 15 are currently working in the field.

Understandably, this partnership takes great pride in its achievements to date, which is only just beginning. In a joint press release they stated, "The partnership between CCEB and Chevron has developed into a relationship that goes beyond the usual grantor/grantee collaboration, and can serve as a model for other nonprofits, local businesses, and corporations to contribute to improving the lives of the communities in which they operate."

The favorable media coverage from such cross-sector partnerships can range from coverage in a local newspaper to garnering publicity across the world. This free media coverage builds strong community goodwill, attracts new employees, increases brand recognition, and helps counter possible negative feelings or publicity. Of course it must be understood that as staff/volunteer time is required to develop and present the stories to the media.

Benefits Nonprofits Receive From
Partnering With a For-Profit Organization

Before I provide the list of nonprofit benefits, I wanted to show the following cartoon by Brian Narelle, who also created our firefly Glow and other graphics for this book. I voiced my opinion that many nonprofit executives needed to explore new ideas and proven ways to raise funding and decrease costs by joining hands with their for-profit brethren and form cross-sector partnerships. A few days later in the mail I received the following cartoon which graphically depicted the opportunity.

Now this is certainly an oversimplification of the situation, but the truth is, if you want to catch fish, you need to go where the most fish are. And they are found in the ponds, streams and lakes that haven't been heavily fished before.

If you think about the areas that nonprofits, especially small and midsized nonprofits, tend to be weaker, it's communications, marketing, technology, some of the things that they can't invest in at that level. These are the assets the corporations have in abundance.

Jeanne Bell, CEO, CompassPoint

As we have seen, there are 38 benefits, and counting, which can be received by for-profits through cross-sector partnerships. Nonprofits are right behind with the potential to have at least the 31 benefits – those we have discovered so far. Here are the top 10 benefits nonprofits can receive and a closer examination into several of them:

Top 10 Benefits

1) Increase funding

2) Connect to new business partners and strategic relationships

3) Receive pro bono services

4) Attract loaned executives

5) Attract in-kind donations (equipment, furniture, computers, software, etc.)

6) Provide professional development for employees

7) Attract new volunteers

8) Provide volunteer management

9) Increase media coverage and improve media relationships

10) Develop earned income opportunities

Increase Funding

In the majority of cases, the primary reason a nonprofit organization seeks a partnership with a for-profit organization is to increase their donations. Indeed, many nonprofits believe the terms "partnership" and "sponsorship" are interchangeable, and they definitely are not. Cross-sector partnerships are focused on developing long-term, multifaceted relationships. The very good news is that these partnerships can, and in most cases do, provide significant financial benefit. And because they are partnerships, the financial benefits should continue over many years.

Receive Pro Bono Services

Pro bono publico, usually shortened to "pro bono" is a phrase derived from Latin meaning "for the public good." The term is generally used to describe professional work undertaken voluntarily and without payment as a public service. Pro bono service, unlike traditional volunteerism, uses the specific skills of professionals to provide services to those that could not normally afford to hire such an agency. For example, the law profession has a longtime tradition of providing such pro bono services. Happily, pro bono services have expanded well beyond the law, opening a lot of opportunity for your organization.

While this pro bono opportunity may be sought in nearly any area of business, where it has become most prevalent is in the creative services. Public relations and advertising agencies, graphic design firms, web designers, copywriters, photographers, artists, nearly all creative agencies are looking for opportunities to promote their work, while at the same time wanting to help their community. Many creative people and agencies gain new clients through the exposure they can receive by working with nonprofit organizations. It is an enormous and free resource for you to tap.

Note: Taproot Foundation is a nonprofit organization that makes business talent available to organizations working to improve society. Taproot has become the nation's largest nonprofit consulting organization and is building a global pro bono marketplace. Taproot has published a new guidebook on pro bono practices: *Powered by Pro Bono: The Nonprofits Step-by-Step Guide to Scoping, Securing, Managing, and Scaling Pro Bono Resources*. Find this book on Amazon and other locations.

Find much more about the Taproot Foundation at *www.taprootfoundation.org* and in the **Resource Center**.

Attract Loaned Executives

An area similar to pro bono services is what is referred to as "Loaned Executives." In my experience I've seen very few nonprofit organizations take advantage of this opportunity. Now this category is not the people serving on your board of directors; that's a very different role. Nor are they your everyday volunteers. Loaned executives are paid by their sponsoring organizations, not the nonprofit. Loaned executives are very skilled, high-level advisors who come into your organization and work on specific areas, typically for periods of three to six months, and sometimes longer.

A good example of a Loaned Executive program was developed by the United Way of the Bay Area. UWBA describes their program as offering "a unique opportunity for Bay Area professionals to give back to the community, while providing their employers with an "out-of-the-box" way to cultivate the next generation of company leaders." These loaned executives, several from Wells Fargo Bank and California Department of Transportation, spent three months working full-time at United Way in responsibilities such as fundraising, delivering presentations and coordinating events at Bay Area companies that participate in United Way programs. All of the loaned executives were sponsored by their company who paid for their salaries and benefits while they worked at the United Way.

These programs provide many benefits to both the person who provided their services and also back to their sponsoring company. In particular, there is the opportunity for professional development of the executive and for an in-depth understanding of the nonprofit sector. This is a win-win situation, for sure.

You might be thinking: That's all well and good for organizations as large as the United Way, Wells Fargo, Caltrans, and the like... but what about me? Rest assured - the opportunity of loaned executives can work for any size organization. Let's say you are a small nonprofit organization that collects warm coats to donate to homeless shelters in the winter. One of your key areas of concern is the collection, storage and distribution of these coats. You could go to a local company that had a distribution process, such as a local grocery store, trucking company or possibly your local UPS. Ask them if they could lend you an executive who could work with you to make your organization's collection, storage and distribution system work more effectively. You might ask your local hardware store if they could lend somebody to help you with inventory management. The list of potential support is nearly endless. You may not get such a loaned executive for 4-6 months, but you probably will get someone who can bring you the expertise you need at no cost.

Attract In-Kind Donations

It may seem a no-brainer that corporations, or any business for that matter, might donate used computer hardware, software, supplies, , furniture, or a myriad of other items that a nonprofit organization could put to good use. Overstocked items, and in many cases, the regular products that a company has or produces might also be donated to your organization, instead of a cash donation. This latter example is the staple of many special events when organizations receive wine, beer, other beverages, food, and related supplies in lieu of cash.

If an organization uses vehicles to take food to shut-ins, provides transportation for seniors, for emergency services or other transportation uses, there is a very good chance that on the back or side of these vehicles you will see the names of for-profit organizations or foundations which have provided funding for those vehicles. Corporations and independent foundations can be approached to support your transportation needs, but don't overlook local new or used car dealerships, trucking companies, delivery services and other local companies that use a lot of vehicles as a potential partner. The prominent sign recognizing the donor on the back of the nonprofit's bus provides a very public acknowledgment of that donor's contribution and promotes its business as well. Remember that the maintenance of these vehicles is quite costly, so take that into account when seeking donated vehicles. Clearly, the best part of in-kind donations is that everything that is donated is something you don't have to pay for. One note here: while many organizations may provide services, these services cannot be taken as a tax deduction, unlike products or supplies. So be sure to check with a tax accountant on this issue.

The best approach is to look carefully at all the line items in your annual budget, in every area of your budget, and see which items or services might be donated from local vendors rather than purchased by your organization. You might be surprised at how much you can save through in-kind donations directly related to your normal cost categories.

Consider in-kind donations as the equivalent to cash, and provide equivalent recognition to the donor. If the donor provides $2,500 worth of in-kind donations to an annual gala, they should be recognized at the same level in your promotional materials as if they gave a $2,500 cash donation. In-kind donations offer several opportunities to a nonprofit organization. Not only can they reduce the expenses and provide supplies or equipment that could increase your productivity or comfort, the request alone could be the beginning of a larger and deeper relationship with that in-kind donor. As with volunteer activities, such simple requests are excellent ways to begin strong partnerships. And all you have to do is ask!

Develop Earned Income Opportunities

A local church invited me to come and discuss ways they could increase their revenue. Now this particular church sits on top of a hill with a spectacular view of the San Francisco Bay. During our discussion it came up that a major telecommunications company had approached the church and wanted to put up a cell phone tower in the back of their parking lot. The tower would take up very little space and would be cleverly disguised as a tree, so it would fit in with the many trees that bordered the church property. I became quite interested in this opportunity until I was told that they declined the offer. Being a church and thus a nonprofit organization, they reasoned they could not have a business relationship with a telecommunications company.

They were shocked when I explained that many nonprofit organizations had business relationships with for-profit companies and indeed, many nonprofits ran their own for-profit operations. Probably the most well-known example is Goodwill Industries, which runs retail stores of donated items. Or that the Girl Scouts sell cookies; Delancey Street Foundation owns and operates the highly popular Delancey Street Restaurant; the Red Cross and other blood centers collect and sell blood to help cover their operating expenses. The practice is very wide-spread. How much so? The National Center for Charitable Statistics estimated in 2008 that nearly 70% of the $1.4 trillion generated by nonprofits came from the sale of goods and services.

The law generally holds that a nonprofit can make money by renting or selling products or services and other profit-generating means, though some of this income may be taxable. According to the NEO Law Group, "The IRS categorizes earned income into two categories: related and unrelated. A public charity generally does not pay taxes on related income, but it does pay taxes on unrelated business income at the corporate rate, also called the unrelated business income tax (UBIT)." So this is a question for your accountant or tax expert.

In the case of the church, it could have legally rented that space for the cell tower, assuming it complied with city laws for the placement of a cell tower. This was a huge missed opportunity, especially when you consider that the rental income of the small space in the back of their parking lot would have exceeded their pastor's annual salary!

Earned Income Case Study

The American Red Cross Bay Area chapter, dead center of earthquake country, wanted to raise funding and spread awareness about the need for having emergency supplies in homes, cars, and places of work. I came up with the idea of doing a "magalog", which is a cross between a product catalogue and a magazine. I envisioned this as a 16-page, four-color magazine with engaging stories about Red Cross disaster operations, a volunteer's story from Hurricane Katrina, helpful "Did you know?" tips, and suggested emergency supplies, which the reader could order through the magalog.

As this magazine/catalog would be released in November, we named it "Give the Gift of Preparedness" for the holiday season. We planned on mailing the catalog to over 60,000 Red Cross donors, and we formed a partnership with *Benefit* magazine who agreed to insert the catalog in their November issue that went out to over 50,000 upscale subscribers in the San Francisco Bay Area. There was just one major problem: we didn't have the internal budget to design, print and mail all of these catalogs.

So we approached one of our chapter's lead partners, Wells Fargo Bank, and offered a partnership opportunity. Together we came up with a program which in return for their $50,000 donation we would print our original printing estimate (110,000) plus an additional 200,000 copies which they would distribute to every Wells Fargo Bank branch location in the San Francisco Bay Area for the public to take home. And we provided the back cover for their partnership advertisement.

We contacted our Red Cross emergency supply providers and offered them the "opportunity" to advertise in this unique emergency preparedness magalog. We raised over $84,000 in sponsorship and advertising funding (2.5 times the cost to design and print) before the magalog was even sent to the printer! So our share of all the sales of the emergency supplies advertised in the magalog was pure profit.

It is estimated that nearly 1,000,000 people read this unusual and very important safety information. It was a huge marketing, emergency preparedness and fundraising success, and all the partners and advertisers were thrilled.

So if nearly 70% of all income generated by nonprofits comes from the sale of goods and services and your nonprofit is not at least exploring this area, look again at the opportunities of earned income. You may be leaving a ton of money on the table!

Volunteers: The Lifeblood of Nonprofit Organizations

Volunteers are not only listed twice within the top 10 benefits; they permeate the entire relationship between a nonprofit and for-profit, especially when you include board members, pro bono services, and

other benefits where personal time and services are being offered free of charge to the nonprofit. In many cases, volunteers are the lifeblood of nonprofit organizations.

When I first joined the American Red Cross, I was stunned to learn that 96% of the Red Cross staff is volunteers. The number of volunteers participating in a disaster relief response can be extraordinarily high. For example, Red Cross sent over 244,000 volunteers to the relief efforts for Hurricane Katrina - that's more than the attendance at the last three Super Bowls combined.

The American Red Cross has developed sophisticated, thoughtful and effective programs to recruit and manage such a huge number of volunteers. The Red Cross gives their volunteers major responsibilities, provides on-going training and evaluation, and keeps them accountable, and on task.

62.8 million adults volunteered almost 8.1 billion hours through nonprofit organizations in 2010.

Points of Light Institute

Match the Task to the Talent

It is important to try to engage volunteers at their level of expertise, and ideally to even push them a bit to enhance their learning opportunity. Bobbi Silten at the Gap Foundation said, "I feel much more competent helping with strategy with a nonprofit than I do painting a fence. I am not competent painting a fence. Some of us have hidden talents." She continued, "Our employees get a lot out of being in this (volunteer) program, not only in what they are able to give but what personally they are able to get. They are more likely to come back if they're feeling good about what they're doing, they see someone benefitting, but they are also building their own leadership skills."

One-Day-and-Done Volunteer Events

One-day volunteer events, such as those provided by Habitat for Humanity or Rebuilding Together, are short projects, such as painting a home, refurbishing a school classroom, planting a community garden. They provide a "try it and see if you like it" opportunity, but with no real commitment. These events are highly popular as teambuilding activities, especially for corporate employees. Having painted a mural at an elementary school as part of Rebuilding Together, I experienced firsthand the camaraderie, hard work and sheer joy of working together for a good cause we all experienced.

However, there are times when these one day and done events can be problematic. John Power, Executive Director of the Volunteer Center of San Francisco, provided the following example: "For many years for-profits have called upon their nonprofit relationships and said, "We want to bring 100 employees next Saturday and have a meaningful volunteer opportunity at your organization." This situation creates tension for both the for-profit pushing for the one-day event and the nonprofit which may be ill-prepared with such short notice to provide any meaningful activities for the for-profit volunteers." Fortunately, this situation can be easily avoided by longer-term planning and close communication between the nonprofit and for-profit organization.

One of the current trends in volunteerism is the move away from these traditional "one-day-and-done" events. Power stated, "More and more companies are interested in delivering greater impact both to the nonprofit and to their employees, so they are more interested in getting more skilled, longer-term opportunities. For-profit organizations need to understand what the nonprofit needs and help the nonprofit expand their understanding about what the for-profit needs."

One-day-and-done events are good. However, their effects tend not to last long enough to create fundamental benefits to the partnering organizations. On the other hand, cross-sector partnerships provide a much deeper, longer-lasting relationship, and thus much more effective morale building and team development benefits for all involved.

Volunteer Management

A major mistake made by many nonprofit organizations is that they accept volunteers based on the sheer fact that these individuals want to help their organization. While very well-meaning, a volunteer without training and especially without on-going support and supervision can become a drain on the organization's staff time and resources, or worse. Running a successful volunteer program requires a well thought-out plan and the capacity to manage the plan.

Consequently, all volunteers should be treated as though they are new employees. In seeking and managing a successful volunteer program it is recommended that you:

- Write a job description for each position with the responsibilities and tasks you want them to perform.

- Recruit your volunteers as though you were looking for new full-time or part-time employees, possibly using Craigslist, classified, online jobsites and other methods of recruiting.

- Thoughtfully and thoroughly interview all applicants, following closely the job description you provided.

- Train new volunteers in the mission of your organization and their responsibilities.

- Hold the volunteer accountable for the tasks to which they are assigned.

- Provide a supervisor responsible for managing them and encouraging them at all times.

- And here's the most challenging part: if they don't work out... fire them!

Yes, they are volunteers and not being paid; however, they are holding responsible positions and are accountable to your organization for those positions. If they are not working up to your expectations, they are probably not that engaged in your mission, and consequently, it best serves both the volunteer and the organization to part ways as soon as possible.

When volunteers are recruited, well-trained and dedicated to your mission, they become active and engaged stakeholders in the success of your organization. By providing such volunteer management, you will increase your efficiency and expand your services, and you can decrease, sometimes significantly, the amount of money that your organization needs to raise.

I want to repeat that last line: You can decrease, sometimes significantly, the amount of money the organization needs to raise through effective volunteer management.

The TCC Group, based in New York City, provides strategic planning and management consulting services to foundations, nonprofits and the corporate community. TCC is one of the leading organizations on measuring organizational effectiveness. Peter York, Senior Partner and Chief Research and Learning Officer, made a presentation at the 2010 Bay Area Volunteer Leaders Forum. He provided the results of TCC Group's study measuring organizational effectiveness around the management of volunteer programs. Peter said one the most startling statements I've heard in a long time: "Nonprofit organizations could lower their annual funding requirements by 20% to 40% if they effectively manage their volunteers."

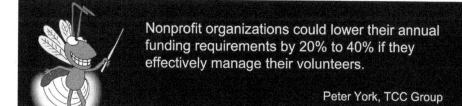

Nonprofit organizations could lower their annual funding requirements by 20% to 40% if they effectively manage their volunteers.

Peter York, TCC Group

20% to 40%! Say you have an annual budget of $300,000, you could potentially save $60,000 - $120,000 per year by effectively managing your volunteers. Wouldn't you consider that amount the net result of an excellent fundraiser, or couldn't that amount cover at least one or two much-needed new staff members? Now if that amount, 20% to 40%, seems like a stretch for your thinking (even though TTC's experience shows that it's not), what if you achieved a 10% to15% net savings? That might certainly make up for the probable drop in your organization's donations over the past several years...and potentially, much more. Now do the same math with your annual budget. It's an eye-opening exercise.

The volunteer opportunity is a huge win-win for the nonprofit and the for-profit, but only when the volunteers are well-managed. For more information, visit TCC Group at: *www.tccgrp.com*

The Volunteer Bottom-Line

When you have clearly defined what you need in terms of volunteers, next develop job descriptions for these volunteer positions, train them well, decide who they will report to, how they will be managed and communicate other important operational issues and requirements of their job. This initial effort on your part will return ten-fold benefits to your organization and also establish relationships, and preferably partnerships, that can serve your organization for years to come.

Volunteers provide great value to your organization, and great value to themselves and their sponsoring organization. The following section addresses the topic of comparative value - people versus money.

Which Provides More Value: Money or Brains?

When considering a cross-sector partnership, not surprisingly, the first topic that seems to arise is money. How much should the nonprofit ask for or how much should the for-profit consider donating? While money usually enters the conversation at some point in a partnership discussion, it's short-sighted to think that money is the only or even the best value to receive in a partnership. Quite simply: If you focus on money you may leave a lot of money/value/assets on the table, never to be seen again.

Karen Baker, California Secretary of Service and Volunteering, offers: "A million dollar value of brainpower is so much more helpful than a million dollars. I can find money. I look for talent and I mean top-shelf talent, which you can shop for when you're shopping for public/private partnerships."

This belief is echoed by Dannielle Campos, Senior Vice President and National Philanthropy Program Manager for the Bank of America Charitable Foundation. Dannielle said, "When working with a nonprofit it can't be just about the dollars but also about the other human resource capital you can bring if that company is interested in making, really building a strategic partnership with a nonprofit in their community. The dialogue has to be bigger than the check and the nonprofits usually need more than just money."

Here is the underlying secret to success of cross-sector partnerships: first seek brains…and the money will follow.

Cause Marketing: Where It All Started for Me

In 1975, Marriott Corporation hired me from my position as Public Relations Director of Cedar Point Amusement Park in Sandusky, Ohio, and sent me to Northern California to be the Public Affairs Manager of their new theme park Marriott's Great America. Marriott had purchased 556 acres of old pear orchards in Santa Clara. This location was dead center in the middle of what was soon to become the world's technology center -Silicon Valley- though we had no clue at the time.

My job was to develop the public relations, press relations and pro-

Photo courtesy of Marriott Corporation

motion for the opening of what was the largest investment in the history of Marriott Corporation. I was 25...and I was jazzed.

Shortly after my arrival, I received a thick document of standard operating procedures detailing how Marriott opened a new property. Their experience was based mostly on hotels and restaurants, not an entertainment complex the size of a small city. I was instructed to spread around free tickets to the theme park, primarily to nonprofit organizations, the press and community groups. This was a "goodwill gesture" to help demonstrate Marriott's desire to be a good neighbor in our new community.

Marriott at that time had no company-owned hotel or name presence in northern California. So it seemed to me that if we were going to have any significant impact or attention, we needed to do something that would stand out. And passing around a few free tickets was not going to do it.

I thought that if we developed a partnership with a nonprofit organization which had a great reputation all over our marketing region, and especially, with an organization that could take advantage of working with us on such a mammoth project, together we could create something special. I had absolutely no concept of cause marketing at the time as this form of cross-sector partnership hadn't been invented yet.

Our small staff started interviewing nonprofit organizations that had a significant presence in northern California and the western United States. One of these interviews was with Chapters West of the March of Dimes. In our discussion I discovered that the March of Dimes had three main goals:

- Increase the number of pledge-walkers

- Increase the overall donations

- Have the donations collected by their campaign's budget deadline

The goal for our team was straight-forward: open the largest project to date during Marriott Corporation's history and attract over 2 million visitors to our new entertainment complex the first year. If accomplished, that would be a new attendance record for a regional theme park.

Marriott's Great America and March of Dimes felt that by working together we could meet each other's marketing objectives. So we formed a partnership.

In March of Dimes chapters throughout their 17 state Western Region, Marriott's Great America provided a grand prize in each region for the pledge-walker who brought in the most money by the deadline. In cities further away from Santa Clara, the grand prize was tickets for their family and plane fare to Santa Clara for the theme park's opening day. However, in the cities that were a relatively short distance to travel, we offered the winner 100 free tickets to the opening day of Marriott's Great America. Needless to say, word of this contest spread like wildfire, especially through middle and high schools of the closer-in cities. This partnership and contest created tremendous visual, viral and media promotion.

The marketing opportunity for Marriott's Great America was sensational. Its name, logo and theme park information were on every pledge card, every poster, every piece of promotional material and press information throughout the Western Region. We utilized our "spokes-rabbit" Bugs Bunny to lead several of the major walks and to do a rather outrageous press tour

The results of this partnership were off-the-chart. March of Dimes raised $2.5 million, 40% more money than had ever been raised in their Western

Bruce and Bugs Bunny on press tour in 1976

Region. And that was a lot of money for a fundraising drive in 1976. Marriott's Great America received hundreds of thousands of dollars in free publicity, word-of-mouth promotion and brand awareness, which was instrumental in attracting a record-breaking attendance of over 2.2 million people in the theme park's first year. Talk about win-win!

According to the Cause Marketing Forum, Huffington Post, Wikipedia and others, this partnership is considered the first cause marketing campaign in history, though the term "cause marketing" hadn't been invented yet. Seven years later in 1983, American Express developed a promotional program for the restoration of the Statue of Liberty and coined the term "cause-related marketing" as part of their campaign.

The irony in cause marketing, as in all forms of cross-sector partnerships: the more you focus on the greater good and not just on making money, (usually) the more sales and donations you will make. While it seems we cannot turn on the TV or open a newspaper without seeking some form of a cause marketing campaign, the market is far from saturated. There is enormous potential in utilizing cause marketing to benefit your for-profit or nonprofit organization, especially in the more local, more personal campaigns, where the utilization of cause marketing is just beginning to grow.

Cause Marketing: What It Is

Cause marketing is a specialized subset of cross-sector partnerships, and like all cross-sector partnerships, cause marketing is a partnership between two or more sectors. Though in cause marketing, the partnership is primarily between nonprofit and for-profit organizations and is primarily about marketing, sales, fund development and increasing brand awareness. Cause marketing has grown by leaps and bounds, and in 2012 an estimated $1.7 billion was spent in North America alone on cause marketing campaigns.

Cause marketing is a marketing campaign with specific strategic goals and objectives. It is not an event, sponsorship or one-time project and certainly not philanthropy. You will find as we explore further into this area that a well-strategized and well-developed cause marketing campaign will bring you many of the benefits we have discussed in cross-sector partnerships.

While there are many definitions of cause marketing, the following is how I prefer to define it.

Cause marketing is a partnership between two or more nonprofit and for-profit organizations whereby each party receives benefit toward their individual marketing objectives, while striving through their combined resources to create a greater good.

Let's break this definition down to see why this particular description is a bit more comprehensive, and possibly more demanding among others available, yet touches upon the foundational elements of highly successful cause marketing campaigns.

Partnership: Going into the partnership, both sides should come together as equals. This equality is necessary for a fair, trusting and successful working partnership. Without this trust, without this focus on true partnership, your campaign is dead in the water before it's launched.

Two or more: In most cases, a cause marketing partnership is between two partners, but as we have seen, sometimes partnerships can have three and even four sectors involved. And sometimes, even multiple partners within sectors. Bringing multiple partners together can leverage the success of the marketing objectives. So don't limit your partner opportunity thinking. More may be better, or maybe not, based on your marketing strategy and campaign needs.

Individual marketing objectives: All sides may be approaching this partnership with very different marketing objectives and internal agendas. This is to be expected. Having clear communication and understanding about these separate agendas and objectives and then working toward the benefit of all partners will greatly enhance the overall success of your cause marketing campaign.

Combined resources: Possibly more than in any other marketing or promotional endeavor, the successful execution of your cause marketing strategy and resulting campaign creates a whole far greater than the sum of its individual parts. You just can't possibly accomplish alone what you can do working together for your mutual success.

Create a greater good: This is the part of my definition that seems to be left out in every other definition I've ever seen. However it is this focus on the greater good that sets the foundation for your successful campaign. Focusing on the greater good is the key ingredient that will motivate all partners and stakeholders involved in your campaign. The greatest impact, the real magic, comes when your campaign focuses on the people, issues or environment that will benefit from the campaign:

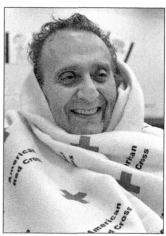

Photo coourtesy of Gene Dailey

- Those whose lives will be saved because they are now prepared for an emergency

- The women and men in the future who will not get breast cancer because of the research you are helping to fund

- The homeless who will be given shelter

- The children who will be saved from starvation

- Addressing serious environmental situations

This is the greater good. You can address any nonprofit's cause, but to be optimally successful, you must focus on who or what will benefit from your effort. Nonprofits as such are not causes in and of themselves, but facilitators that bring much-needed services and support to the cause, which of course, is the people, environment or social issues themselves...the greater good.

Types of Cause Marketing Campaigns

Cause marketing campaigns come in all shapes and sizes - from national campaigns such as the Pepsi Refresh Project, designed to fund good ideas, big and small, that help refresh our world - to a local barbershop supporting St. Baldrick's Foundation to raise funding for children's cancer research, and every conceivable application in between.

Cause marketing campaigns fall into one or more of the following categories:

- Pinup or Point-of-Sale

- Purchase-Triggered

- Action-Triggered

- Donation-Triggered

- Behavioral Change

- Social Media

- Cross-Media/Integrated Media (sometimes called Transmedia)

The type of cause marketing campaign decided upon depends greatly on what an organization needs, the type of partner(s) chosen, and the capacity and resources the partners bring to the table.

Pinup or Point-of-Sale Campaign

You see these all the time when you walk into a grocery store. The person checking you out at the cash register will ask you if you'd like to make a donation to a particular cause, which is added to your bill. Children's Miracle Network and St. Jude Hospital are two very popular pinup campaigns. When you make a donation, you write your name on a paper plaque, which is usually posted on a store window. The store collects all the donations and forwards them to the charity. This campaign gives you an immediate "feel good" as your plaque is posted. Kids love this one, of course. The customer donation is usually small, $1-$2.

The perfect example of this type of cause marketing campaign is the annual Halloween Promotion benefiting St. Jude Children's Research Hospital, one of the world's premier centers for the research and treatment of pediatric cancer and other catastrophic childhood diseases.

During the month-long Halloween Promotion, thousands of restaurants, convenience stores, grocery stores and other retail locations nationwide encourage consumers to make a $1 donation to St. Jude. In return for their contribution, donors write their names on pumpkin-themed pinups, which the establishments display throughout the month of October.

Many point-of-sale campaigns avoid the pinup aspect altogether and just have the donation added to the bill, such as Safeway's fundraising campaign for breast cancer, which also eliminates the need and cost of the paper plaque. Safeway has raised a total of $108 million for breast cancer awareness and research.

A program growing in popularity is Hotels that Help (www.hotelsthathelp. org), which encourages hotel operators to add a $1 contribution to their final hotel bill. You can, of course, opt out of

Point-of-sale pinup for St. Jude

providing this donation, but the vast majority of people leave the $1 donation on the bill. The management and employees of each hotel decide which local or regional nonprofits will receive these donations. The one dollar donation against a significantly higher hotel bill makes for a relatively easy choice, and hotels and their employees enjoy the opportunity of benefiting their community.

Such pinup and point-of-sale campaigns are especially effective because customers are asked directly for a donation when their wallets are out, and the donation is usually small. The only real downside to pinup campaigns is customer and check-out person fatigue. It's difficult for the store personnel to ask every single customer for a donation and do so enthusiastically, at least after the first 100 or so customers. This can be partially mitigated by strong management encouragement, visits from the nonprofit personnel, contests or bonuses for the most money raised, and not having the campaign last more than a few weeks. Frequent customers can get tired of hearing the same pitch for the same cause. And sadly, customers sometimes react badly to the poor guy/gal behind the register who is trying to help the cause or just doing his/her job.

Overall, pinup and point-of-sale campaign can be quite successful. Millions of dollars have been raised by the largest programs, and they can work especially well for local charities which serve people in the surrounding area of the retail store and where there may be a more local/emotional appeal to the cause. However, in order to manage expectations here, pin up campaigns tend not to raise a lot of money unless they are undertaken by national organizations such as St. Jude, Safeway, Children's Miracle Network and the like, utilizing hundreds if not thousands of locations. But these campaigns are still quite valuable and provide great branding and community relations opportunities for the nonprofit and for-profit partners.

Purchase-Triggered

Another form of cause marketing campaign is what's called a purchase-triggered donation. That's when the customer buys a product or service and a donation is made to the cause being promoted. My favorite example of a purchased-triggered campaign is TOMS Shoes.

With every pair purchased, TOMS will give a pair of new shoes to a child who has none. Using the purchasing power of individuals to benefit the greater good is what TOMS is all about. This concept, which they call "One for One" (buy one and give one away) is a

Photo courtesy of TOMS Shoes

growing trend in cause marketing. As of September 2010, TOMS had given over 1,000,000 pairs of free shoes... and that was a while ago!

AT&T has a highly successful cause marketing relationship with Special Olympics in many markets around the country. In a promotion that ran from May 2011 to Feb. 2012, AT&T donated $40 for every new activation of any product listed on their co-branded website by an AT&T customer. Some form of this AT&T promotion has been going on for many years.

Purchase-triggered can also refer to when you dine out during a special promotion where a percentage of your meal's cost is donated to a charity. You pay for the meal and the restaurant makes the donation.

Purchase-triggered donations work very well for smaller cross-sector partnerships, whether it's a local store providing a buy one, give one program, a restaurant's charitable contribution, buying insurance from a local agent, purchasing a new car, providing a job referral or the almost unlimited ways that nonprofit contributions can be made from the sales of any product or service.

Action-Triggered

Who hasn't been involved in some sort of cause campaign where you run in a half-marathon or 3-day benefit walk or pledge to give a certain amount of money for each mile or lap someone else does (my favorite!), like kids raising money for their school for running laps around the track. In these cases, the action of others triggers your donation. Many social media campaigns are also action-triggered campaigns.

The Leukemia & Lymphoma Society's Team In Training is a great example of an action-triggered cause marketing program. Team in Training has trained over half a million runners, walkers, triathletes, cyclists and hikers and raised over $1.2 billion to fund lifesaving cancer research. While this program, the Avon Walk for Breast Cancer, March of Dimes and other similar programs are national in design, the exact same action-triggered concept is frequently used by your local elementary school and local youth organizations.

Donation-Triggered
One Warm Coat

One Warm Coat started out in 1992 as a Thanksgiving weekend coat drive in San Francisco. Since then, more than 3 million coats have been donated during their 20-year history. This terrific program was started by Sherri Lewis Wood and had been originally run out of her bedroom. Only in 2011 did she hire her first full time employee, and yet this campaign has been an unbelievable success and model cause movement all across North America.

One Warm Coat teamed up with the Burlington Coat Factory and ABC TV's Good Morning America for a campaign that runs between October and January of each year. Anyone wishing to donate used or new coats can drop them off at the Burlington Coat Factory locations. As a thank you, donors receive a coupon for 10% off their purchase at the Burlington Coat Factory stores. This particular campaign has collected more than 1,000,000 coats.

ONE WARM COAT
.onewarmcoat.org

Sherri told me, "The partnership is extremely valuable for all three partners because we each

Addison Graham, volunteeer, One Warm Coat

have a different role to play in the drive: Collection (at Burlington Coat factory stores), Distribution (through the One Warm Coat network of agencies) and Communications/Media by ABC's Good Morning America.

A great example of a donation-triggered campaign involves two well-known names: Goodwill Industries and Whole Foods. These organizations partnered to celebrate Earth Day. Goodwill put their familiar bins at participating Whole Foods locations around the San Francisco Bay Area. The goal was to divert used clothes and household items that would otherwise be dumped in landfills. The result: Nearly five tons of clothing and household goods were collected in over just the one weekend of this campaign!

When exploring a donation-triggered cause marketing campaign, it can be helpful to look for particular days, seasons or special events that are already in the public's mind. One Warm Coat takes full advantage of the holiday season because of its gift-giving focus and the fact that in many parts of the country it can be very cold. Other opportunities include Valentine's Day, Halloween, President's Day, or even National Harmonica Day. Tying a campaign to the notoriety and/or emotion of a particular day, season or event can tap into the consumers' existing interests and increase the attraction to the campaign.

St. Baldrick's Foundation began on March 17, 2000, when three business executives decided to turn their annual St. Patrick's Day celebration into a fundraising event to benefit kids with cancer. To make this event more interesting, they decided to have a head shaving event as their fundraiser. Their goal was to raise $17,000 on March 17. But when the clippers stopped clipping over $104,000 had been raised in that very first event.

Since that first event, St. Baldrick's Foundation has established itself as a volunteer-driven charity committed to funding the most promising research on childhood cancers. According to its website, "The St. Baldrick's Foundation currently funds more in childhood cancer research grants than any organization except the U.S. government. Since 2000, more than 246,000 volunteers—including more than 24,000 women—have shaved in solidarity with children fighting cancer at the Foundation's signature head-shaving events around the world. Each shaveesm is a walking billboard for the cause!" Thanks to generous friends and family, these shavees enabled the Foundation to fund more than $103 million in childhood cancer research grants.

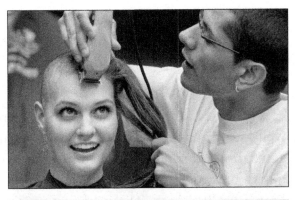

It doesn't get any better than that. What I like best about St. Baldrick's

Photos courtesy of St. Baldrick's Foundation

(besides its great slogan: Shaving the Way to Conquer Kids' Cancer) is how many cause marketing success factors it includes:

1) The cause is highly emotional, raising funds for children with cancer.

2) By having their heads shaved, participants are making a very personal commitment to the cause.

3) The fundraising events are very "local," being held in barbershops, salons, schools and other locations all across the country and around the world.

4) It's a relatively simple event/campaign to execute successfully.

5) It's action-triggered; you must really do something (have your head shaved and raise money to support lifesaving childhood cancer research).

6) It utilizes the high visibility of St. Patrick's Day to enhance the promotion of the St. Baldrick's March events.

Cause marketing works best when people are personally and emotionally engaged in the cause. With St. Baldrick's, hearing those clippers buzzing toward your head certainly gets you engaged and probably a bit emotional as the hair from your very own head falls to the floor. But with each strand that falls, and every dollar raised, the potential to find cures for childhood cancers rises.

Behavioral Change Campaign

The following campaign examples are cause marketing partnerships between a nonprofit organization and/or governmental agency and the media. Such campaigns are designed to have maximum emotional impact and are targeted to a wide public audience in order to change a personal behavior pattern. They usually do not involve a payment or donation.

Vince & Larry, the Crash Test Dummies

A classic campaign designed by The Ad Council focused on getting the public to wear seatbelts and cleverly combined humor with a very serious message. According to The Ad Council, "Since Vince & Larry, the Crash Test Dummies, were introduced to the American public in 1985, safety belt usage has increased from 14% to 79%, saving an estimated 85,000 lives and $3.2 billion in costs to society." View a spot from this clever campaign at: (*www.youtube.com/watch?v=C5h2NF2xMYI*)

Another Ad Council iconic campaign was called "The Crying Indian" and featured the late actor Iron Eyes Cody as its spokesperson. In this Keep America Beautiful public service campaign, Iron Eyes Cody, who portrayed himself as a Native American, is seen standing next to a stream with a tear running down his cheek as he spoke of the

PSA from Ad Council

need to stop littering and polluting our environment. It was first aired, appropriately, on Earth Day.

Changing behavior is one of the most difficult and expensive types of cause marketing campaigns. In many, if not most cases, campaigns that take on major behavioral changes are funded by the government and/or the result of legislation or lawsuits.

In early 2012, The Centers for Disease Control and Prevention and U.S. Department of Health and Human Services teamed up to produce a new anti-smoking campaign. According to their joint press release, "The $54 million campaign will be seen on billboards and print, radio and TV ads that show people whose smoking resulted in heart surgery, a tracheotomy, lost limbs or paralysis."

Highly successful behavioral issue campaigns can also be accomplished with a significantly smaller budget. Take the campaign called Fair Play. Concerned about the health of Marin County, CA, several community organizations partnered with the annual Marin County Fair to create a culture that encourages fair visitors to make healthier choices both at and after the Fair. Fair Play is striving to address and change social norms and provide a healthier and more family-friendly environment at the Fair. They have created changes in policy practices and voluntary measures related to alcohol, tobacco, access to healthy foods, physical activity and healthy living. Because of this effort, all advertising and sponsorship for alcohol and tobacco have been banned at the Marin County Fair. As the saying goes: Think globally, Act locally.

Social Media Campaigns

Without a doubt, the fastest growing area of cause marketing is in the area of social media. It is absolutely exploding. Campaigns abound utilizing the social networks of Twitter, Facebook, LinkedIn, texting and many other online or mobile platforms and applications.

For example, a remarkably swift and effective campaign was launched by the American Red Cross after the devastating earthquake hit Haiti. Two days after the quake, over $4 million had been raised, and that number quickly increased to over $32 million in the month following the earthquake, all from more than three million people using their mobile devices to text "Haiti" to 90999. Each text automatically donated $10 to the American Red Cross. The speed and effectiveness of this campaign was due in large part to mGive, a mobile donation platform, which is a subsidiary of Mobile Accord Inc. donated its services. Of course, the devastation in Haiti and the tremendous international media coverage made it very easy for people to want to help. Texting made it simple.

More recently, the same text numbers and approach were utilized with high success to make donations to the Red Cross following Hurricane Sandy's devastation on the East Coast and Midwest of the United States.

This type of text-to-give campaign can be done at a very local level. For example, Mobile Loaves & Fishes in Austin, Texas wanted to raise awareness of the homeless situation in their community. They devel-

oped a social media campaign called "I Am Here" which focused on one homeless man: Danny Silver. The campaign was promoted on local TV and radio stations and in the local newspaper. The public was asked to text "Danny" at 20222 which would trigger a $10 donation. This campaign raised enough money to get Danny and his disabled wife off the streets and into a home. It also brought great coverage and better understanding of the plight of the homeless population in Austin.

Note: I borrowed (the polite way of saying stole) the "I Am Here" example from my friend and colleague Joe Waters, which was taken from the book he co-authored, *Cause-Marketing for Dummies*. Joe is one of the country's leading experts on cause marketing and also the founder and "chief information pusher" on his blog *www.selfishgiving.com*.

Cross-Media/Integrated Media Campaigns (Sometimes Called Transmedia)

As with cross-sector partnerships, cross-media (or what is also called integrated or sometimes transmedia) can greatly increase the impact of cause marketing campaigns. Integrated media campaigns combine the impact of multiple marketing and media disciplines. A good example of an integrated media campaign combining general advertising, in-store promotion and social media was the matchup of two major brands, Pepsi and 7-Eleven. By purchasing a Pepsi product at 7-Eleven locations, proceeds of up to $250,000 were donated to Feeding America, which provides emergency food assistance to 37 million Americans each year, including 14 million children and three million seniors. Additionally, customers were able to double their donations by visiting 7-Eleven's page on Facebook.

"Studies show that cause-marketing and social media are two critical ways to reach millennial consumers, a target demographic for both 7-Eleven and Pepsi," said Jesus Delgado-Jenkins, 7-Eleven's Senior Vice President of Merchandising, Marketing and Logistics.

Regardless of an organization's size, cross-media/integrated media approaches should be a part of any well-thought-out cross-sector partnership or cause marketing campaign. As is my mantra throughout this book, small and midsized organizations, whether nonprofit or for-profit, can and should take full advantage of every marketing opportunity.

Striking the Emotional Chords

There is no getting around it. When we see an advertisement or public service announcement that hits our emotional buttons, we respond to it, we are drawn to it and in most cases - we remember it. Emotion sells. And there is no reason not to take advantage of the proven effectiveness of an emotional appeal in cause marketing or any cross-sector partnership effort.

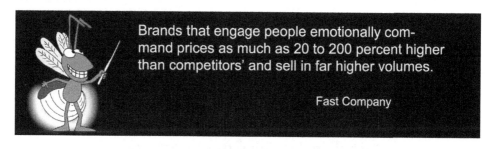

Brands that engage people emotionally command prices as much as 20 to 200 percent higher than competitors' and sell in far higher volumes.

Fast Company

What to Avoid When Developing a Cause Marketing Campaign

Even with the best intentions, sometimes among major players who should know better, cause marketing can go terribly wrong. The mantra of cause marketing, indeed of all cross-sector partnerships, is that the partners need to be well aligned. Their missions, their products or services and how they present their campaign to the public must make sense as a partnership. The public becomes skeptical when they smell or taste that the campaign is purely done to make money. Here are some bloopers.

Kentucky Fried Chicken (KFC) Pothole Program

Recognizing the ubiquitous problem that many of our roads and highways have fallen into disrepair, KFC thought that it would be a good idea if they teamed up with several cities around the country and filled in those cities' potholes. So the public would know who was making this generous donation, KFC painted their bright white logo on top of the freshly laid asphalt. As you see in this promotional photograph,

"The Colonel" is pointing his cane at a recently paved, logo-covered pothole.

So we see potholes filled with oily black tar, covered with a KFC logo, which will be run over by cars, slowly but surely erasing the logo. This message has the unintended effect of linking KFC and its heavily-oiled, deep-fried chicken with steaming oily black tar and inadvertently, brings a whole new meaning to "road kill."

I hate to pick on KFC, but if the bucket fits. After the above-described campaign, they developed a partnership with Susan

Photo courtesy of KFC

G. Komen for the Cure and produced a second highly-questionable campaign where they really stuck their wing in it.

"Buckets for the Cure" Campaign

KFC and Susan G. Komen for the Cure launched a campaign in which they printed pink KFC buckets with the breast cancer ribbon and then handed their customers the bucket full of fried chicken wings, legs and breasts. $.50 of the sale of each bucket went to the charity. What were they thinking? A respected nonprofit organization dedicated to education and research about breast cancer promoting deep-fried food, in pink buckets.

Photo courtesy of KFC

Yoni Freedhoff of Weighty Matters said: "So, in effect, Susan G. Komen for the Cure is helping to sell deep-fried fast food and, in so doing, help fuel unhealthy diet and obesity across America, an odd plan given that diet and obesity certainly impact on both the incidence and recurrence of breast cancer."

What was this campaign really all about? Yes, money. KFC donated more than $4.2 Million to Susan G. Komen for the Cure, the largest single donation in organization's history. Roger Eaton, President of KFC Corporation said, "This was a campaign that allowed our customers to fill up their stomachs and their hearts at the same time." Needless to say, this campaign caused a media and consumer controversy which, if only briefly, damaged the credibility of Susan G. Komen… but it made lots of money.

The investor extraordinaire, Warren Buffett, once said, "It takes 20 years to build a reputation and five minutes to ruin it." There is nothing worth the risk of destroying a hard-earned reputation.

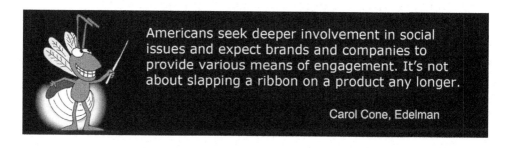

Americans seek deeper involvement in social issues and expect brands and companies to provide various means of engagement. It's not about slapping a ribbon on a product any longer.

Carol Cone, Edelman

The key points I would suggest you take away from this discussion on what not to do in cause marketing:

- Do absolutely nothing that will hurt your brand. Good reputations are hard to gain and much harder to regain if lost.

- Never be just about the money; greed is ugly and hard to hide.

- Always put the cause first, which will gain attention, loyalty and finally, financial success.

- Be unique! Stand out from the crowd! Don't be a chicken! (sorry)

Wrapping Up

Cause marketing comes in all shapes and sizes and can be an exceptionally effective fund development and brand awareness-generating program because it:

- Leverages the marketing clout, assets, intelligence and connections of organizations from different sectors

- Focuses on doing good, and the public responds very well to organizations

- Motivates your employees, customers and all stakeholders of your organization

- Attracts media attention...for free!

- Generates sales and raises donations

- Delivers what one organization can't possibly do alone

Note: You will find excellent research studies and much more on cause marketing in the **Resource Center.**

PART III

HOW TO DEVELOP A CROSS-SECTOR PARTNERSHIP OR CAUSE MARKETING CAMPAIGN

Now you're ready. You understand the importance of embedding a cause consciousness within your organization. You know how cross-sector partnerships and cause marketing will grow and benefit your organization. Whether you work for a junior college, a five-person technology startup, the local chapter of Make -A-Wish foundation, a state government agency or a large nonprofit or corporation, you are prepared to begin your journey to a more effective and profitable organization. You might even have a few potential partners in mind or causes that are particularly important to your employees. As when building a house, no matter how ambitious your plans, without a well-designed blueprint, your house may become just a jumble of wood and nails.

I have seen so many mistakes due to misunderstandings between the sectors - rushing ahead before doing the necessary homework, developing programs and campaigns without the proper resources in place, marketing efforts based on the wrong strategy, money wasted and great ideas that failed because of not wanting to deal with the small details. So we are going to drill down into some detail. OK, a lot of detail.

And one last thing before we dive in - you may think that you don't have the resources, the time, potential partners, or enough relationships in the community or with media to pull this partnership business off. Here I will show you that you can be highly successful if you follow the path and Cross-Sector Partnership Development Process presented here. So step onto the path and start your amazing journey now.

Cross-sector Partnership
Development Process

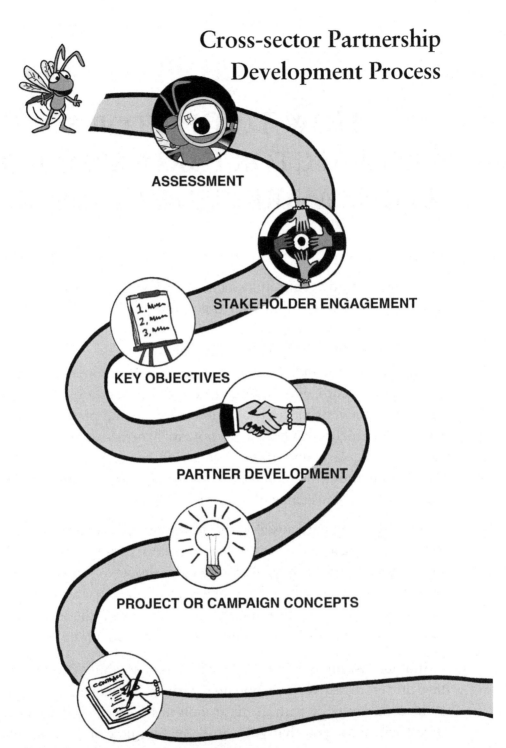

ASSESSMENT

STAKEHOLDER ENGAGEMENT

KEY OBJECTIVES

PARTNER DEVELOPMENT

PROJECT OR CAMPAIGN CONCEPTS

NEGOTIATION / LEGAL / AGREEMENTS

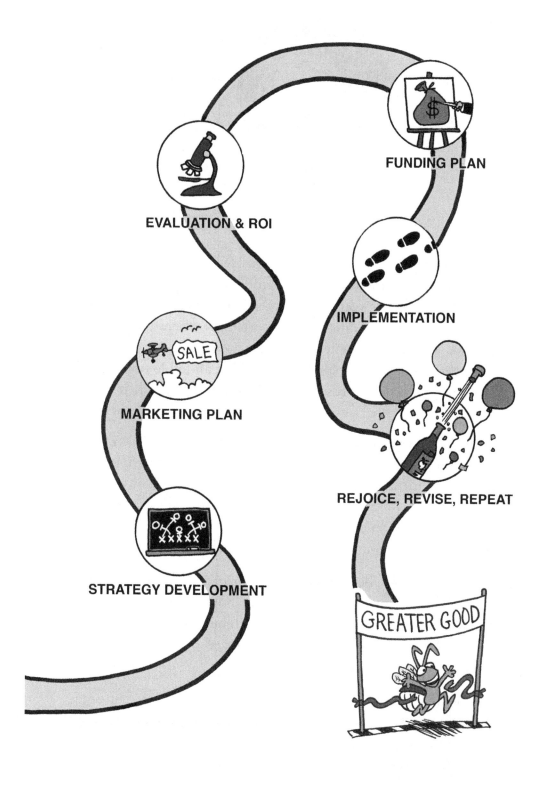

FUNDING PLAN

EVALUATION & ROI

IMPLEMENTATION

MARKETING PLAN

REJOICE, REVISE, REPEAT

STRATEGY DEVELOPMENT

GREATER GOOD

Assessment
Know Thyself!

Before you start your partner exploration process, you need to analyze carefully your reasons for wanting a partnership, assess your abilities and assets, and especially your commitment to deliver your end of the bargain. A clear understanding and preparedness when entering into a cross-sector partnership comes only after a comprehensive internal assessment confirming that you're ready, willing and able to be a productive partner. In other words: you must first know yourself before you can reach out to others.

Who are you? Most organizations think they have a pretty good idea of who they are. They may have vision statements, mission statements, standard operating procedures, annual reports and/or press releases that tout their latest products, services, partners, achievements, etc. However, without analyzing your corporate culture, and especially how you're seen by the public, you may not know who you really are.

Amazon founder Jeff Bezos described your organization's brand as "What people say about you when you're not in the room." Your brand, which is a fancy way of saying your reputation, is not who or what you think you are but how you are viewed by all who come in contact with your organization.

Taking the time to develop a clear understanding of what your organization really stands for and how it is viewed by the public is not only the necessary foundation for a successful cross-sector partnership, but for the success of your business in general.

Before you begin the Assessment Process I present here, I strongly recommended that this process be led by your senior management, preferably your CEO or Executive Director. S/he must be involved in this cross-sector partnership conversation and Assessment Process, at least in the beginning stages, as this individual sets the overall tone, direction and strategy of your organization. I suggest that your Assessment Process team include several people from the list below, though a smaller organization may not have or need this deep a team.

- CEO/Executive Director

- Chief Marketing Officer and/or highest member of your sales or marketing team

- Director of Community Affairs and/or Public Relations Director

- Top representatives from your outside creative agencies (PR/ advertising/marketing)

- Director of Human Resources

- A member of your Board of Directors, especially one whose business is marketing or creative services

- At least one well-respected employee

- At least one volunteer, if applicable

- A recorder: Someone to take detailed notes and serve as the communications link for all on this assessment team

The entire Assessment Process should take no more than two or three meetings, especially if notes are provided and next steps are determined as assignments for each member of the team to prepare for the next meeting. The length of this process depends greatly on the commitment of the team, leadership involvement, and how much work may have already been done by your organization.

In the course of this Assessment Process, problematic issues may arise - be sure to address them immediately. Such issues rarely go away and can be very embarrassing and a waste of time and money if not handled early and well. The key to this critical exercise is to ascertain if your company has the motivation, ability, personnel, budget and leadership to undertake a long-term partnership, with all of its inherent bumps and challenges...and rewards.

The following is the Assessment Process I designed for for-profit organizations. An electronic copy of this form as well as the Assessment Process for Nonprofit Organizations can be found at the **Resource Center.**

Assessment Process for For-Profit Organizations
Step 1: What Do You Want to Do?

Have your assessment team brainstorm and write down all of the ideas and needs that you think would best serve your organization. Here is a sampling:

- Increase your product or service sales

- Introduce a new product

- Attract new customers

- Increase employee satisfaction and morale

- Generate broader brand recognition

- Attract favorable media coverage

- Help in opening a new office or service area

This is a small sampling indeed, as this list could become very long. Undoubtedly, new ideas will be added to this list as you go through the Assessment Process, and certainly when you begin meeting with potential partners, more and more opportunities come to light. But it's good to come to an agreement on the general direction that your organization wishes to follow.

Step 2: Assess Your Company and Brand Perception

With the ability to craft your messages through advertising, sales materials, social media and public relations, all too often organizations see themselves and thus their brand as what they are promoting externally. Nothing is further from the truth. It bears repeating: Your brand, which equates to your reputation, is what others think of you, not what you think of yourself. To miss this key fact is to waste an enormous amount of time and money.

The objective in this second step of your Assessment Process is to understand as fully as possible how your company is perceived by the following groups:

- Your employees

- Your customers

- Your suppliers

- Your competitors

- The industry you are in

- The community or markets where you do business

- The media

- Indeed, anyone and everyone who comes in contact with your company, its products or services

Start Step 2 of your Assessment Process by asking your team the following questions:

- Have you done a survey of the different stakeholder groups listed previously to ascertain your brand perception? What were the results? If you haven't, this is a must-do first step.

- Does your customers' brand perception of your company differ from how you would like to be perceived? How significantly does it differ?

- How do your employees describe your brand and your corporate culture? Have you asked them? If not, it is important to do so.

- How would you/your executive team describe your corporate culture?

- What are your target market audiences and/or segments?

  a) Geographical market areas

  b) Demographics of your customers (gender, age, race, etc.)

- What is your history in working within your community, especially with nonprofit, education or governmental entities? Describe good experiences and challenging ones.

- What do you currently provide to your community, such as event sponsorships, cash or in-kind donations, volunteers, employee matching grants or other services, products or donations? Please detail.

You should have a pretty good understanding of your organization's reputation and brand and will be able to answer most or all of these questions. If you have contracted with external advertising or PR agencies, they will have probably developed an analysis of your brand in their creative development of your messaging. If you do not have such information to answer each of these questions, I suggest you utilize the simple, inexpensive (basic levels are free) and highly efficient online survey opportunities from such companies as www.surveymonkey.com or *www.verticalresponse.com*. For *The Burtch Report*, we used the basic level (10 questions or less) of SurveyMonkey, and each survey was free!

Surveys provide the necessary "snap shot" of where you are and who you are. In order to develop a successful survey for this book, Vivek Bhaskaran, CEO of QuestionPro, has generously provided a step-by-step approach to designing an online survey/questionnaire. His most helpful approach can be found in the **Resource Center** under Survey Development.

Step 3: Is Your Organization Ready for a Cross-Sector Partnership or Cause Marketing Campaign?

This is not a rhetorical question. Even though you fully recognize the benefits to your organization of developing cross-sector partnerships, as with any business venture, you need to assess whether you are capable in staff time, financing, and other areas to take on such an effort. Cross-sector partnerships require a significant investment in time and people to make them successful, though the results should far outweigh the effort.

Questions:

- Have your CEO, Executive Director, and/or other key leaders committed personal involvement to developing a cross-sector partnership?

- Can your organization allocate financial resources to this endeavor?

- Can your organization assign a respected person to serve as the primary point of contact with other partners for the duration of this relationship?

- Does your organization have internal marketing resources with the ability and time to undertake a long-term cross-sector partnership?

- Does your organization have consulting and/or external agencies to help with the creative aspects?

- Does your organization have existing relationships in other sectors with the potential to become partners in a campaign?

- Does your organization have existing partnerships? Or have you ever done such a partnership or campaign in the past? If so, what did you do and what did you learn from these experiences?

- Is your organization willing to form a transparent partnership which allows both/all parties to share information essential to a successful partnership? (This does not mean confidential information.)

The following are a few related issues that need to be addressed to ensure the proper assessment of your potential to take on a cross-sector partnership.

Executive Buy-In

J. David Pincus, author of the book *Top Dog* and a leading researcher in the study of leadership and CEO communication, coined the term "CCO," Chief Communications Officer, referring to the vital dual role the CEO plays in company-wide communication. He commented, "Few, if any, major organizational initiatives have much chance of succeeding without the whole-hearted support of and hands-on involvement by the top executive, for every key constituency takes its cues from that singular individual who is not only the organization's de facto leader but its tone-setter, role model and emotional cheerleader as well."

This critical role as key influencer is not limited to internal audiences only. Pincus continues, "The commitment of an organization's CEO to a particular cause or initiative sends a clear signal to other business and community organizations who may be asked to participate. Potential external partners know the highest level of leadership will be engaged in the endeavor."

Your CEO (Executive Director for a nonprofit, principal or superintendent for a school system, agency director for government) must be the champion of your organization's cross-sector partnership or cause marketing effort. In most cases he or she will not be the on-going "point-person" in the relationship, but his/her message must be clear to all involved: "I am fully committed to this partnership, for the good that it is doing for our organization, our partners, and society."

Time and Resource Commitment

Your partnership team must understand that it will be spending at least six to 12 months in the development and execution of your cross-sector partnership program or cause marketing campaign. Your team and especially your organization's leadership need to be prepared to make that type of commitment.

Logo/Intellectual Property

Your organization has important intellectual property that may include your corporate logo, copyrights, trademarks, marketing slogans and the like. You may have a style guide or other document that provides very clear stipulations on how you can use your logo, your brand, your key messaging in printed or communicated materials. It should go without saying that nothing in your cross-sector partnership should create any negative reactions to your reputation or to your intellectual property.

Anything Else?

The assessment questions and related issues I have provided will cover most of the information and challenges that could arise as you begin to develop your partnership. This list is not exhaustive and other things may come up in the course of your relationship with your own organization and certainly when working with partners in other sectors. Avoid no issue: deal with them right away.

Step 4: What Do You Bring to a Partnership?

Now is the time to take a long hard look at what your organization brings to the partnership. As in a poker game, your chances of winning are far greater if you know what is in your hand before you worry about what's in the hands of the other players.

Develop a detailed list of all the assets, people, support agencies, talents, etc. of what your organization brings to a partnership. Here is a sample list to begin this important assessment. You should be ready and prepared to offer to your potential partnership some or all of the following: begin:

1)   A strong brand, name recognition and reputation – local and/ or beyond

2)   Executives, management team members and employees committed to the success of the partnership

3)   Senior management support for employees to engage in the

programs of the partnership, preferably, paid time off for volunteering hours

4) Employee volunteers interested in participating

5) A valuable service or product to promote, if this is the priority of your partnership; otherwise, you might just want to focus on providing a service to your community.

6) Internal creative services

7) External creative resources, PR/Advertising agency

8) In-kind donations of products, services, equipment, office or meeting space, etc.

9) Business partners that might wish to join and support the partnership

10) Contacts with the media and important influencers in the community

11) Management or employees who could become advisors or board members of partner organizations

12) The sincere desire and commitment to do something good for your community and world

Step 5: Defining Your Partnership Team

This step of the Assessment Process is to define the management and staff personnel who will develop and lead the on-going partnership. In the majority of cases, the on-going partnership team will not include your CEO but it may include a member of your senior management. Small organizations might, however, include their CEO or Executive Director on their partnership team.

Additionally, your on-going partnership team should be made up of:

1) A point-person who will serve as the primary interface between your organization and the partnership. This point-person should report on a regularly scheduled basis to executive management and your partnership team.

This point-person needs to be very well respected at all levels of your organization to be able to accomplish their task efficiently. In most cases, this point-person should be selected from your marketing, community relations or public relations team, as these areas of responsibility tend to require experience in effective communication and dealing with diverse external entities and challenges. You also want someone who has the vision of what might be accomplished and the optimism that it can actually get done. A lot rides on the success of this point-person's role, so choose carefully.

2) A member of your human resources or employee volunteer management team. These people bring an important perspective of the personnel and abilities within your organization.

3) An employee whose area of responsibility relates to the project/ ideas under consideration.

4) If feasible, a member of your external public relations and/or advertising agency. As professionals in the area of community relations, creativity and media relations, they bring a wealth of ability, important contacts and external experiences to the team.

This five-step Assessment Process is the strong foundation upon which your future partnerships will be based. Take nothing for granted, do this homework, and make any changes necessary if this Assessment Process exposes deficiencies in your communications, your organization and/or your brand. Indeed, one of the great benefits of this process is uncovering other important issues to be addressed that might not have anything to do with the development of an external partnership.

Once this Assessment Process is complete, you will feel much more confident and competent as you begin your search for the right partner(s).

Stakeholder Engagement Utilizing Your Full Team

Wikipedia defines a stakeholder as: "Any person, group, organization, or system who affects or can be affected by an organization's actions." Look around at all the people who are involved in your organization, both internally and externally: your employees, your customers, your shareholders, your vendors, your community, your business partners, government regulators, the media - these are your stakeholders and these are the people who really matter. These are the people you must protect, serve and value the most. When you focus your efforts on bringing value to all your stakeholders, you create the greatest beneficial impact for your organization. The converse is also true – if your stakeholders are not engaged, not valued, they have the potential to have a negative, and sometimes significant, impact on your organization.

Here is a diagram that illustrates the many stakeholders of a typical for-profit organization.

The stakeholders for a nonprofit organization are very similar. Your shareholders are your donors, your customers are the people you serve, your business partners are your volunteers, etc.

As you see, there is an interrelationship, indeed interdependency, where all stakeholders are involved in a give-and-take relationship with the organization of which they are stakeholders. At first glance, it would seem that the relationships are primarily between the organization and the outer circle of their stakeholders. However, as this

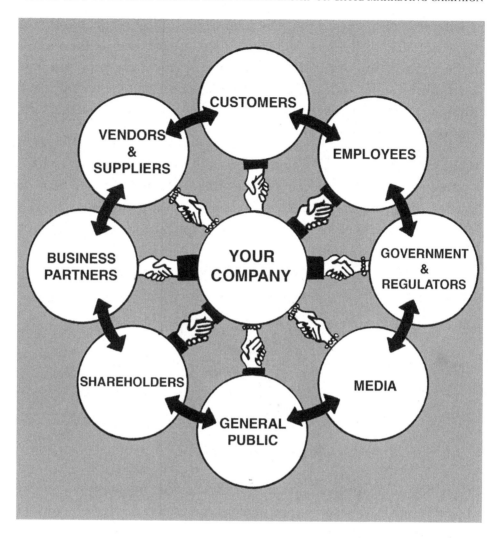

diagram reflects, the stakeholders themselves can have separate relationships between themselves, and thus impact and influence the entire organizational ecosystem.

As we explored earlier, when an employee believes that their organization has a particularly strong commitment to being a good citizen in their community, they will loudly and confidently communicate this belief. Consequently, the stakeholder and communication/effect cycle is potentially more interrelated. The ramifications can be significant, as any positive or negative influence a stakeholder has on other stakeholders can have a corresponding positive or negative influence on the organization itself.

The very good news is that when an organization is focused on the success of all stakeholders, all stakeholders are focused on the success of the organization. And when an organization is focused on not only benefiting all stakeholders, but additionally in serving the greater good through a well-designed and well-executed cross-sector partnership, your organization will begin to glow.

Your stakeholders will provide an honest critique because they have a vested interest in the success of your organization. They will provide creative input, business contacts, perhaps funding, and a myriad of other assets that will serve your cross-sector partnership endeavors.

Key Objectives

Before beginning the deep dive into what your organization would like to do through a cross-sector partnership and then defining your key objectives, there is a critical first step - asking the question: Do you know your WHY? The products or services your organization provides is the what you do. The manner in which you deliver these products or services to your customers or the public is how you do that delivery. However, the most important question that you and your organization must determine is why you do what you do. The why must come first. The why is your driving motivation. It's what inspires you, your employees, your donors, indeed all your stakeholders, to take interest in your organization and to support it wholeheartedly. Without a strong and articulated why, you are just another nuts-and-bolts organization (in any sector), and one of the very many.

The similarities to what we have described as a glowing business are

obviously related to the why. Glow starts from within, and radiates outwardly, and so does the why. You can't have a glowing organization unless all your stakeholders are inspired and motivated, thrilled to be involved and thrilled to tell others about this involvement. My belief is that the best and maybe the only way to create this glow, this why, is by embedding a cause consciousness into the very essence and culture of your organization. When your organization stands not just for your own benefit, but far more importantly, for what you can do for others and to create a greater good...that's the glow, that's the why.

Simon Sinek wrote the terrific book *Start With Why*. He writes, "By WHY I mean, what is your purpose, cause or belief?" And further on, "People don't buy WHAT you do, they buy WHY you do it."   And my favorite line: "… all those who share the organization's view of the world will be drawn to it and its products like a moth to a light bulb." Or in our case, a firefly!

With the understanding of your WHY firmly in place, now you can move on to what you want to do. We have explored the multiple benefits that can come from a cross-sector partnership. But practically speaking, your organization must choose the specific objective or a very short list of priorities that are the highest priorities. For example, you may decide that your top priority is to raise the sales revenue of a particular product or service, provide employee volunteer opportunities in your community or to open up a new store or business location. If you are a nonprofit, your primary objectives may be to increase your donor base, fund and open a new project or program, attract corporate volunteers, develop an earned income opportunity, etc.

To assist in determining your "What do you want to do?" process, you may wish to utilize the two "Top 10" lists: *Benefits a for-profit organization can receive by working with a nonprofit organization* and *Benefits a nonprofit organization can receive by working with a for-profit organization*, provided earlier in this book, or preferably, review the complete lists of benefits which can be found in the **Resource Center.**

Now you have over 30 distinct benefits your organization may be able to receive in a cross-sector partnership and these will serve as a guide in determining which objectives would have the greatest positive impact on the needs, challenges or opportunities facing your organization. When developing your strongest case for what will work best for your organization, and in due course what will provide the best partnership opportunity, you need to select from these ideas or objectives your top three, and then very clearly, define and agree upon your number one objective.

Have your team answer these questions:

- What is the number one objective that would have the greatest impact on our organization? This top priority may be all you need for the focus of your campaign. Clearly define it in one sentence.

- If you have a second objective, define it but make it second in your effort.

- If you have a third objective, define it but make it third in your effort.

By defining your top objectives, and especially by selecting one as your top objective, you significantly increase your potential for a successful project or campaign. If you try to address too many objectives you will weaken the energy, resources and talent, and potentially not accomplish any of your objectives.

Partner Development
Let's Go Exploring!

Before we start off on our exploration for partners, there is a critical concept - alignment- that must be well understood. The correct alignment between your organization and a potential partner is of paramount importance and must be the filter through which all of your discussions, meetings and decisions are viewed. By alignment I mean that when put side by side, your brand aligns with their brand and your values with their values so that this partnership is intellectually, emotionally and practically compatible. It must make sense to the partners and especially to the public. This critical need for the proper partnership alignment is also referred to as "brand fit."

As we saw in what I feel was the stunningly poor example of brand fit between Kentucky Fried Chicken and Susan G. Komen in the "Buckets for the Cure" campaign, the wrong product or service alignment can be disastrous for a cross-sector partnership or cause marketing campaign, and more importantly, to an organization's reputation.

In your Assessment Process, you looked at your brand, what your organization stands for and the reputation of your company in the marketplace. This is the starting point of your alignment process. Appropriate brand fit is fairly obvious. If you are a grocery store, for example, an appropriate brand alignment would be to work with your local food bank or a homeless shelter. If you are a construction or hardware supply company, Habitat for Humanity or Rebuilding Together would provide outstanding alignment because your business expertise, employee talents and your knowledge of construction materials are needed in the building or remodeling of homes.

This alignment creates a natural flow when integrating the mission and cause of your partners into your own organization's culture. It just makes sense - to you, to your organization, to your partners, to the public - to all you wish to attract to the cause.

Here are two examples of excellent alignment:

An Appetizing Trio: Campbell's Soup, Susan G. Komen for the Cure and Kroger Stores

This campaign goes back a few years but provides one of the best examples I've ever seen of the right brand alignment and a gusty creative idea involving one of the world's most recognizable brands. This three-partner campaign did an amazing thing: it took the 140-year-old iconic red and white brand of Campbell's soup, changed it to pink and white, and added a pink ribbon. For the one-month campaign, they placed these pink and white cans in 2,500 Kroger stores, a major Midwestern supermarket chain. Kroger promoted the fundraising/awareness-raising campaign throughout the region of each store, but most importantly, the in-store displays drew exceptional attention to the new pink cans and naturally, to the cause. Campbell's donated 3.5 cents for each can that was sold to Susan G. Komen. During this one-month campaign, sales of Campbell's soup doubled in the 2,500 participating Kroger stores. As the success of the campaign began to grow, many store managers set up additional displays of the pink and white Campbell's soup cans outside of their normal location in the soup section, increasing exposure and thus creating additional sales.

In its first year, this cause marketing promotion generated sales of over seven million cans of Campbell's soup, which netted approximately $250,000 to the charitable organization. Importantly, the seven million cans of soup went into homes and reinforced the partnership message of supporting breast cancer research. It doesn't take a marketing wizard to realize that when you have such a successful campaign, you should do it again. So the following year the partners executed basically the same one-month campaign in the 2,500 Kroger stores and sold over 14 million cans of Campbell's soup!

A Daring Duo: Barefoot Wine and Surfrider Foundation

A more recent example of excellent brand fit or alignment is the partnership between Barefoot Wine and the Surfrider Foundation, whose mission is the protection and enjoyment of oceans, waves and beaches. Together they created the Barefoot Wine Beach Rescue Project to help keep America's beaches "barefoot friendly." The partnership hosted beach cleanups and restoration events coast-to-coast, utilizing volunteers to clean the shorelines, plant native greenery and collect litter along the beaches. At the end of each event, volunteers enjoyed Barefoot Wine and surf-inspired food. Aligning a brand like Barefoot Wine with the surfing-originated and water-focused Surfrider Foundation is an example of excellent alignment. Even the events themselves emphasized this barefoot-friendly fit.

The campaign won the Cause Marketing Forum's 2012 "Halo Award" for Best Environmental or Animal Campaign. And while the campaign and both organizations are national in scope, this type of cause-related campaign could just as well have been orchestrated with any community park, beach or swimming pool partnering with local businesses related to water sports. It's about finding the right idea and the right brand fit.

Finding a Partner

Everyone is going after the Fortune 500 corporations or the top 50 nationally-known charitable organizations. The competition at this level is fierce, for their attention and a potential partnership. In most cases, I advise against jumping into that fray. However, if you have a fairly small organization (in any sector) in a fairly small community, you may not have many sizable organizations to choose from. Don't let that stop you. There are plenty of great but smaller partner opportunities to work with and they usually will be much easier to approach

OK, now is the time to put on your most comfortable hiking boots, pull out the well-worn jeans, clean the old binoculars and fill the water bottle - you're about to go exploring. Be confident, you are fully prepared to enter the wonderful world of cross-sector partnerships. We are going to explore how to find a nonprofit partner and how to find a for-profit partner. This exploration works just as well when seeking partners from the education and government sectors.

"Established For-Profit Seeks Nonprofit Partner for Mutual Opportunities"

While it's not quite as easy as placing a classified ad, you are on the search to find a partner to help provide the business objectives you are seeking. You are also about to undertake an out-of-the-box experience and educational journey. There is so much to learn and so much to enjoy as you reach out into the nonprofit and educational communities or even seek a government partner. With approximately 1.6 million nonprofit organizations in the United States alone, there are bound to be one or two that best match the criteria of your search.

Involve Your Stakeholders

A great place to start your partner exploration is with those people closest to your organization. I suggest that you hold an all-staff meeting (even if there are only two to three people "on staff") and invite a board member, a few customers, friends in the media, volunteers, business partners, etc. Begin this session by clearly stating the following key factors supporting your decision to seek a cross-sector partnership.

- The results of your Assessment Process, so that all employees/ stakeholders understand the work that has been done, and especially, the CEO/leadership commitment involved in developing a cross-sector partnership program.

- The why of this effort. You must communicate why a partnership is important to your organization and most especially, why you feel a partnership will benefit those whom the nonprofit organization serves - the greater good. It is the why that attracts others to your cause.

- The what: The one to three top objectives you have selected. Keep them in their proper order, though be flexible in case something comes up in your partnership search that might, for very good reason, reorder your objectives.

- Use the list of benefits as a guide to explore as many potential benefits as possible.

The purpose of this meeting with your internal team and others is to begin the process of developing a master list of your best potential partners, and once those are determined, narrow your focus down to your top three and no more than five best candidates. Before selecting March of Dimes as our best partner with Marriott's Great America, we reviewed approximately 20 regional nonprofit organizations, selected our top five, interviewed three, and selected the organization which best met our mutual marketing objectives. Fortunately, March of Dimes agreed with our selection.

Other Resources for Seeking a Nonprofit Partner

What may have come out of the above processes is not a particular nonprofit but possibly an area of interest or cause, such as working with underserved children, providing shelter for the homeless, supporting a particular cancer treatment or medical ailment. Also take advantage of the several online resources which will help guide and narrow your search.

UniversalGiving.org

UniversalGiving.org is an award-winning website and 501(c)(3) nonprofit organization that helps people give and volunteer with the top-performing projects all over the world. All projects are vetted through

UniversalGiving's trademarked, proprietary Quality Model™ and 100% of each donation goes directly to the cause. This site is easy to use and provides opportunities to donate and volunteer with nonprofit organizations all over the world. Importantly, they do the due diligence on these organizations so that you know they have met UniversalGiving's stringent requirements.

CharityNavigator.org

This is also a great site to find organizations in your areas of interest. It breaks down nonprofit organizations by categories such as human services, health, environment, education, arts and culture, animals, etc. In addition to providing detailed information, it also provides a rating system, from one to four stars, with four being the top rating. I have found Charity Navigator's presentation format easy to follow and understand. The search box at the top of the Charity Navigator works best if you know the name of the charity, and like UniversalGiving, you can type in keywords such as your subject area and location and find a multitude of organizations.

GuideStar.org

Guide Star is another terrific resource for finding detailed information on nearly every nonprofit in the United States and beyond. You will find the leadership of the organization, detailed descriptions, and importantly, copies of each nonprofit's 990 IRS forms. One of the benefits of working with 501(c)(3) nonprofit organizations is that they must submit this 990 form tax document annually to the IRS. These forms allow the IRS and the public to understand how nonprofits operate and provide detailed financial information. Reviewing these forms gives you a clear view of the financial stability of the organization and also how they spend their money.

GuideStar works best when you know the name of the particular organization you are seeking. However, you can use their "Advanced Search" tab to search by subject matter.

Local Resources

If you are seeking nonprofit partners that are more local in nature, especially organizations that might not be affiliated with national charities, many area Chambers of Commerce will have nonprofit listings on their websites. Many cities also provide local business and nonprofit listings. For example, in my county of Marin, California, the website Marin.com provides a comprehensive community listing of nonprofit organizations and businesses.

Other organizations, such as volunteer centers and foundation centers, can be found online and in most major cities, where an enormous amount of information has been gathered. It's free in most cases. These centers usually have libraries that provide publications, printed and online directories, and other valuable information.

Consider What the Public Finds Most Appealing

While popularity is certainly not the most important factor when determining which organization, project, cause or issue would provide the best focus in selecting a nonprofit partner, knowing that an issue has strong consumer interest should be taken into consideration.

For the past five years, Edelman, the world's largest public relations agency, has conducted a Goodpurpose® study. According to the Edelman website, this annual global research study "explores consumer attitudes around social purpose, including their commitment to specific societal issues and their expectations of brands and corporations." The 2012 survey was conducted in 16 countries among 8,000 adults. The following graphic from the study provides a ranking of what consumers care most about.

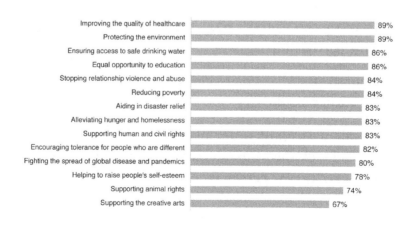

Improving the quality of healthcare	89%
Protecting the environment	89%
Ensuring access to safe drinking water	86%
Equal opportunity to education	86%
Stopping relationship violence and abuse	84%
Reducing poverty	84%
Aiding in disaster relief	83%
Alleviating hunger and homelessness	83%
Supporting human and civil rights	83%
Encouraging tolerance for people who are different	82%
Fighting the spread of global disease and pandemics	80%
Helping to raise people's self-esteem	78%
Supporting animal rights	74%
Supporting the creative arts	67%

A Word of Warning

As part of your due diligence in exploring potential partners, be on alert for areas of potential controversy. For instance, some organizations have an exceptionally high cost of fundraising as compared to the money they put into their services. This can be a turnoff to the media, the public and to funding sources you may wish to partner with. Guide Star and Charity Navigator have rating systems and other information on this overhead/fundraising to services provided cost ratio. And always conduct a web search on the organizations you are exploring, looking especially for any media coverage that might be negative. If there has been any controversy in the recent past, it is usually a good idea to avoid a partnership with this organization until its reputation improves.

Have no doubt; you will find several organizations that fit the criteria you're seeking. So by all means, choose partners that enjoy the highest reputation, solid management and are void of controversy. The partnership should reflect well on all parties.

"Attractive Nonprofit Seeks Motivated For-Profit Partner for Long-Term Relationship"

Oh, if it were only that simple. The steps and criteria when you are a nonprofit organization wishing to set up a partnership with a for-profit company are nearly identical as a for-profit seeking a nonprofit, educational or government partnership. Your partnership development team should:

- Undertake the Assessment Process

- Define your top one to three business objectives in seeking a cross-sector partnership

- Hold a brainstorming session to develop a short list of potential for-profit partner candidates

- Communicate with all of your stakeholders the business objectives and seek their input as to appropriate for-profit partners and particular personal contacts they might provide

Web Search

Having completed the above steps you will have a preliminary list of potential candidates, and you may add to that list as your investigation for the best aligned partner candidates continues. With this list in hand, read their website, especially looking for employee volunteer activities, community relations or corporate social responsibility sections, mission statements, messages from their leadership, their annual report and press releases. Also search the web to find anything and everything that's been published in the media, industry associations and other information about the organization. Again, keep a sharp eye out for anything that might be seen as controversial.

To expand your search beyond this initial list, do an online keyword search using city, area of interest, and other criteria and you will be able to find for-profit organizations that fit the parameters set up by your partnership development team.

LinkedIn

If you are not currently a member of the web-based, primarily business-focused database LinkedIn, I recommend that you join immediately. There is no cost for the basic service and there is an enormous amount of information on people and companies that will serve your partnership search. Once you have identified particular companies of interest by searching LinkedIn, you will find profiles of executives working for that organization and you may find people within your network who are connected directly to those executives. If you are provided with a particular name, the LinkedIn "Profile" will provide an excellent background on that person. It is a very helpful source for information and networking.

Hoovers.com

Hoovers is a subsidiary of Dun & Bradstreet, a business research company. Hoovers provides detailed information on most for-profit organizations in the United States, if they are of any size. They offer a free level of service which provides basic information such as location, address, telephone number, key executives and a short list of their primary competitors. In most cases, there's little reason to pay for a higher level of service.

Business Journals

Another good source is the Business Journal or Business Times which are published weekly in larger U.S. cities. And many communities will have a business-focused magazine. Many of them publish an annual *Book of Lists*, which is a comprehensive compilation of the largest 50 to 100 companies in a myriad of business categories, such as largest public companies, largest private companies, fastest growing, etc. *The Book of Lists* will provide the organization, area of business, address, telephone number, CEO and other pertinent information.

In many cities, the Business Times/Journal will also publish an annual *Giving Guide*, which highlights the major philanthropy and non-profit work within their community. This is a great source for finding out which nonprofit organizations are receiving funding from for-profit companies. It will offer profiles and other information to guide your understanding of these partnerships, and provide ideas for your own partnerships.

Of course, the business section of your local newspaper is helpful, especially if they have online search capability, though I have found business journals and these special editions to be more targeted and easier for finding a lot of information quickly.

Chambers of Commerce

Most communities of some size will have a Chamber of Commerce, and if you go to the Chamber of Commerce's website, most of these websites will list a "Member's Directory" and present all the members of their Chamber, usually by the category of their business, such as banks, attorneys, printers, PR/advertising agencies, and the like.

These listings will usually give you the name of the organization, address and a website, though rarely have I found they provide the key person or their email. Again, if you find organizations of interest but have no direct contact, one or more of your stakeholders may know a member personally and provide an introduction.

Volunteer and Foundation Centers

Utilizing a volunteer or foundation center can be highly productive, as there is so much information in one location, and many times the center will have subscriptions to fee-based services, which they will provide free to you. They also have paid and volunteer staff trained to help you.

Focus Your Search on the Marketing Department

The budgets of a corporate marketing and sales department are between 100 and 1,000 times larger than the budgets of their foundation or their philanthropic giving. Consequently, it is in the marketing and sales department that you will find the big partnership money, and your largest opportunity.

As an example, the Gap Foundation, which is highly effective in developing strong community improvement efforts, provides approximately $1 million a year in community funding. By comparison, Gap Inc. spent over $70 million in advertising for the Gap division alone in 2010, and the overall advertising budget of Gap, Inc. (which includes Gap, Old Navy, Banana Republic and other retail brands) exceeded $115 million in 2003. I would presume this spending has gone up significantly since then, thus the Gap Foundation budget is far less than 1% of their combined advertising budget.

The marketing department provides other overall business and sales strategies for the for-profit organization. And in most cases, the sales department, public relations department, public affairs and community relations departments reside within the marketing department. So open this door first.

Seeking an Educational Partner

There is little argument that our school systems are in dire need of support, especially in lower- economic regions or sections of our larger cities. As we discussed with Art from the Heart, so many children are without art or music programs, and also physical education classes and other activities many of us grew up with in our schools and took for granted. The lack of these programs is devastating on the creative and physical development of our children. Partnerships with the education sector provide the opportunity to do good for our schools and our youth in schools, and such partnerships can create an emotional impact and attractiveness for funding, media coverage, interpersonal engagement and other valuable benefits to all partners and stakeholders involved. In other words, schools are right and ripe for partnerships. Here are two examples of innovative cross-sector educational partnerships:

Hire for Education

Hire for Education was a partnership developed by the recruitment process outsourcing company Accolo (www.accolo.com). When an individual or organization provides a referral for a job opening through their online system, Accolo will provide a donation to your school. All you have to do is put the school's reference number in their online system for the donation to be activated. It's simple, highly effective and profitable for schools.

Kohl's Cares

Kohl's, a department store chain, won the Cause Marketing Forum's 2011 Halo Award for educational program. Kohl's launched the *Kohl's Cares $10 Million Contest*, which awarded $500,000 to the top 20 vote-getting schools for a total of $10 million. Facilitated by Facebook, the contest asked customers, parents, teachers, school supporters and students, "What would your favorite K-12 school do with a half million dollars?"...and then opened the entries up for online voting.

I'm not a fan of such contests (popularity or audience size-focused) where you vote for your favorite...unless there are thousands of winners. However, this particular contest/campaign enrolled 82% of eligible schools in the country, again demonstrating the serious need for funding.

These are just four examples of local, regional and national educational cross-sector partnership programs and opportunities. The potential of forming partnerships to support our schools and the resultant benefits to the partners is seemingly endless. And, needless to say, the schools are waiting for your partnership.

Seeking a Government Partner

The competition for government-funded grants is extraordinarily challenging, as much or possibly even more than seeking funding from corporate or independent foundations. Taking funding out of the equation, what is many times overlooked are the multiple opportunities for cross-sector partnerships utilizing the knowledge, reach and influence that working with the government can provide.

Fishing in the City is an excellent example of how the California State Department of Fish and Game was able to establish multi-sector partnerships, bring their information (and fish!) into classrooms, and provide an educational experience for all involved. While they brought much to the table, they didn't bring funding. That was provided by the other partners involved in the program.

Karen Baker, California Secretary of Service and Volunteering, has instigated several innovative programs bringing the private, nonprofit and public sectors together. She knows that government could play a much larger role than it is now providing. "What's really missing in this (partnership) discussion is the role of government, but the limitation is that government (financial) resources are scarce. What I'm also equally intrigued by is people really don't know how to get into the public (government) sector space as a partner. Most of the professionals that I've met have only done the private and nonprofit deals."

Adding government's non-financial resources to your partnership can greatly expand your reach and influence. Don't overlook this opportunity.

Focusing on Your Best Potential Partners

At this point you will have a short list (three to five maximum) of nonprofit, for-profit, educational or government partners that seem to best fit the criteria of working with you in a cross-sector partnership. Preferably, you will be able to reduce that list to your top two or three organizations so that you can concentrate your information gathering. You might have easily found one particular organization that seems to stand out and meet all of your partnership criteria. However, this immediate match-made-in-partnership-heaven is rare. I strongly recommend that you investigate at least two or three potential partners at this stage.

Do not rush forward to set up an in-person meeting with these potential partners, either. First you need to focus your alignment lens and make sure you have pulled together and analyzed all the information you can find about these organizations. It is critical that you do this analysis first and avoid potential problems, financial and otherwise, that may arise as you get further into your partnership discussions.

These two or three organizations should meet the following criteria:

- Their organizational mission is well-aligned with your organization

- They reasonably match your organization in size and marketing region

- The organization is not controversial

- The organization is financially stable, preferably successful and growing

- The organization has a primary audience (age, gender, geographical, interests, etc.) that is the same or similar to your organization or the audiences you want to address

- The organization is one with whom your team would be excited and passionate about forming a long-term, strategic partnership

When you have done your homework and feel right about a potential partnership with these selected organizations, you will radiate the enthusiasm that says you're about to enter a win-win relationship. I cannot emphasize enough the importance of this preparation, the confidence it will give you and how beneficially this positive attitude will influence the potential partner sitting across the table.

Developing a Partnership

The partner development process is nearly identical for all sectors. If an example presented here speaks more to the for-profit sector, just imagine the same situation from your own sector's perspective, and vice-versa.

Approaching Your Potential Partners

Now that you're confident in your two or three best candidates for partnership, begin the approach process. Ideally, in your discussions with your employees and other stakeholders, you have been given the names of high-level contacts at these potential partners. The very best approach is to ask your contacts to set up a three-way, in-person meeting with their contact at each of the potential partner organizations. Don't be shy about this – you want an in-person meeting, or at the very least, a three-way telephone conversation to begin the process. In asking your contacts for an introduction, make sure that they have a clear understanding of why you want to meet this particular person and what the value will be to the contact's organization. Your contact should be enthusiastic about you and your organization so that this enthusiasm will transfer to who they are contacting on your behalf.

In most cases, this is purely a "get acquainted" meeting, so it's best that this first meeting is just the three of you. It's less formal and more comfortable to look each other in the eye and see if there's any chemistry or reason to go forward with your potential partnership discussions. It's best if you go to your potential partner's organization for this meeting, or meet in a neutral place, like the local coffee shop.

A Suggested Approach

Plan carefully how you want to approach your personal contact to ask for her/his help. Don't take chances with this and just shoot from the hip. You have too much to lose if your contact is not enthusiastic and knowledgeable about your ideas or desire for their help.

Here is a suggested opening of a conversation with your friend/ contact:

Hi Sue. I have some very exciting news. It hasn't been announced publicly yet, but we are going to open up a new Ramos Building and Supplies store in Cleveland. We don't have a store there, and we want the Cleveland community to know that we are going to be good neighbors and good community citizens, as we have been in our other locations. I know that you're friends with one of the board members of the Shelter for the Homeless chapter in Cleveland, and I read that they are opening a new shelter. I think there's a wonderful opportunity for us to provide volunteers from our new store and some building supplies to this great organization, but I don't know anyone there. Could I ask you the favor of setting up a meeting between your friend on the Board or with their executive director and myself? And would you please attend this meeting? Having you there would show that we're very serious about working with them.

Sue will have more questions and you will go into a bit more detail. However, when she makes the call to set up a three-way meeting she will be enthusiastic knowing that this new store could be very helpful to the nonprofit organization in Cleveland. She will want to help you... and the board member and/or executive director will be looking forward to the meeting, knowing that there is good potential value in it for their organization. You are set up for success even before the first meeting.

A Word of Caution:

When asking for this meeting, your friend/contact may say, "Just drop my name and I'm sure they will meet with you." This is an easy way for your friend/contact to believe they are helping you without really getting personally involved. But, they must get personally involved! From my experience, this "drop my name" approach rarely works. And indeed, the higher level you go, the less successful this not-so-personal approach becomes. Having your friend/contact personally set up and attend this first meeting not only guarantees that you get the in-person or over the phone meeting, but most importantly, your contact serves as your advocate for the beginning of a trusting relationship between the organizations.

How Much Time Should You Ask For?

I have found these first meetings have lasted anywhere from 20 minutes to an hour and a half, so ask for 30 minutes. By asking for 30 minutes you are being respectful of their time, and this respectful approach will help get you the appointment.

How much time is enough, or what is too much? Several years ago an associate and I had a meeting at Sun Microsystems to introduce a new service opportunity. In setting up the appointment I had asked for 30 minutes. At the 25 minute mark, I could tell that my associate thought that we should wrap up our discussion. However, our Sun counterpart was fully engaged in the discussion, so we continued. At 45 minutes, my associate closed her notebook in what I thought was an inappropriate way of saying, "It's time for us to leave." I looked over at our counterpart and said, "I see that we have gone considerably past the time I had requested and I want to honor this time commitment." To which she said, "No, I want to understand more about this offering... let's continue." We left after an hour and 15 minutes, and it was a very successful first meeting.

When You Don't Have a Personal Introduction

Getting to the right contact at an organization is always the most challenging part in beginning your partnership search. If you don't know anyone personally and your stakeholders or friends aren't able to provide an inside track to a key executive as a good partner candidate... here is a proven technique that I use.

If the company is fairly large, I will go to their website and look for the "Investor Relations" or "Press Relations." Many times this will be a separate section or might be listed under the section "About Our Company." Usually there you will find a link to recent press releases and in most cases, at the bottom of that press release there is a press contact name, an e-mail or telephone number. This person may not be the person that you eventually want to talk to, but this person knows everybody at the executive level of their organization because they write and sometimes speak for the organization's executives. In the vast majority of cases you will find these people to be quite friendly and helpful. After all, you don't put mean people in your public relations or media department!

Be sure to prepare a few key points that you wish to discuss with them about your interest in their organization, and especially, the value you can bring to them. Write these points down and have them ready for your conversation. The faster you get to the value you can bring them, the more likely they will keep you on the phone and eventually, help you. You do not want to read a script to them, but pretty close to that. Rehearse your opening so that it comes across naturally.

Here's an example of a good opening:

Hi Tomas, This is Janet Moore, Executive Director of Shelter for the Homeless in Cleveland. I just read that Ramos Building and Supplies is going to open a new store here. I believe your employees would benefit from working hand-in-hand on a new community project we are developing. The local TV station has already requested an interview about it, so I know this project is going to receive great press coverage.

Would you be able to give me the name and direct telephone number or e-mail of the person in charge of community partnerships?

Right up front you're telling this person you are bringing something of value to their organization. They will likely realize that you may be helping the public relations and media relations with this potential relationship. Do not talk about the needs of your organization at this point. If for some reason they're not clear on who might be the best person to provide a contact, suggest the director of marketing, director of public relations or director of community affairs.

There is the possibility that you might be connected immediately to the right contact. I'll never forget the time I was connected by their media person on this first "cold call" to the office of the CEO of a major corporation... and the CEO answered the phone! Luckily I had prepared my short pitch and had practiced what I was going to say. So once I got over my brief shock... I went into my reason for wanting to set up a meeting. He said he was interested in this opportunity but that I really needed to talk to his director of community relations. And get this: He would have this person call me... and she did. WOW!! I could've messed up this wonderful opportunity if I had not been prepared.

Another time, I was trying to find the marketing director in Northern California for a major mobile phone company, and I couldn't find the person's name, title or contact information anywhere I searched. So I did an Internet search and found out that their corporate headquarters was in Dallas, Texas and their corporate phone number was listed. I called the main number in Dallas and asked to be connected with their director of marketing for Northern California. She asked me to hold, and in a matter of a few seconds I was transferred to that marketing director's cell phone, in Northern California....and she answered! This was amazing. The only problem - during the call I had to politely ask for her name!

So start with the media relations/public relations people because they are usually not the executive gatekeepers (those who are paid specifically not to let you talk to the executives!) and being far enough from the executives, they're usually more willing to give out internal information and hopefully connect you directly to the right person.

A word of caution: If you are a nonprofit organization contacting a for-profit organization, in many cases you will hear, "There is a grant application form on our website you need to fill out first." Stop...do not go there, unless as a last resort. You must communicate that this is not a donation request. Gently explain that you are not looking for funding or a sponsorship but that you have a business partnership opportunity you think would work best for their public relations or marketing department. You must have your pitch ready and practiced to get around these challenges.

Remember: Any open door into the organization is the right door. If for some reason you strike out finding a good contact name, another great entry point at most organizations is their Human Resources

(HR) department. And in many cases, it is the HR department that directs employee relations and their community involvement. So definitely check them out.

Send a Personal Letter of Introduction

If you don't have a friend/contact who can set up a personal meeting, and you haven't been able to gain entry through more unconventional approaches, at least you should now have the name, title and address of a high-level contact as your potential partner. The next best approach is to send a short letter to this contact. Yes, a personal, on real paper stationary with a stamp, letter. When was the last time you got a personal, stamped and signed letter? Didn't it get your attention? Rarely do people send letters anymore because e-mail is so easy. But e-mail is impersonal, especially to someone you don't know. If you want to grab their attention and show you have an important proposition that will bring value to their organization...send this personal letter. To make a good first impression, this introductory letter must be short, no longer than 10-12 short sentences.

When I was developing a marketing and partnership program for the USS Potomac Association, which owned Franklin Delano Roosevelt's 1936 presidential yacht, we had stationery featuring the official Presidential Seal. You can imagine the impact this envelope and stationery had when it hit the desk of the recipient, with its red, white, blue and gold embossed presidential insignia! Your stationery might not be quite that impressive, but I assure you it will be far more impressive than an e-mail.

Here are my recommendations for a successful introduction letter:

- The opening line must grab their attention by talking to the value that you can bring them. This will keep them reading. If you are being referred by someone, absolutely use that reference as your first sentence. Be sure to say why he/she feels you and this person should get together. Your opening should be something like: "Last year a partnership we developed with Rebuilding Together generated a 20% increase in donations.

I would like to explore…" Once you have grabbed their attention, move into why you feel the alignment between your organizations makes sense.

- In your research, you have chosen these potential partner organizations because they seem to have a good alignment with your organization. You know their key messages and what their CEO or Executive Director has been saying in the media or in their press releases about their organization's role in their community. So, in your message you want to show a strong alignment between your organization and what they are saying with their public messaging. Ideally, you want to parrot back to them what they are saying, without ing the exact words. You will sound in line with their philosophy because you are saying what they have already said.

By the way, do not mention that you are talking with other organizations. That question might come up when you are in a face-to-face meeting, but at this point it could be negative to your efforts.

- Tell them why you want to help, the problem you're trying to address, such as the need for the community to have a new homeless shelter. Briefly explain why your organization might be uniquely positioned to help make this shelter happen.

- Tell them a little bit about your organization, and if possible, something that has been successful that would relate to what is important to them. This should only be two or three sentences max.

- If you are a nonprofit approaching a for-profit, you might want to emphasize that a relationship with your organization would be most attractive to your local media, would create strong community awareness of their involvement, serve as a fun project and morale boost for their employees, or other realistic benefits.

- End the letter with a specific request, a call-to-action. I can't tell you how many times I have seen letters, e-mails or other pitches that have no call-to-action at the end. It's like a car salesman telling you all the benefits of the new car model, then never asking you to buy it. You must close the deal, even if the deal is just to get that first appointment. So at the end of your message or letter, ask for a specific appointment time and suggest a few specific ones that work for your schedule. For example: "Would you be available on June 17, any time between 9-11:30 a.m., or on the 18th during the same time frame?" Offering this time frame will help reduce the all-too-often back and forth scheduling challenge. And it might make your contacts immediately look at their calendar, which is exactly what you want them to do.

Note: This first letter is not and should not be a proposal. It is way too early to get into detail, so do not overwhelm them with your ideas. You have one goal: to get a personal face-to-face meeting. You do not want to give them any reason to say, "I saw your proposal and I'm not interested." And this reaction will happen many times if you put too much information and ideas into your introductory letter. Most importantly, never put a dollar amount in this letter. At this early point you really have no idea the best financial relationship between your organizations.

In many ways, this letter is a tease, and the more concisely written, focusing on a couple of key points as to why you feel this partnership is well-aligned and brings benefit to their organization, the better the chance of your arousing their interest and getting that all-important face-to-face meeting.

I have put a sample letter in the **Resource Center** for your review.

When All Else Fails...Send an E-Mail

Of course, the far less attractive approach is sending an e-mail. The problem with e-mail is that busy executives receive an enormous amount, and the higher the level of the executive, the higher the probability they have an administrative assistant/gatekeeper who monitors all e-mail coming in. This person decides what is important for the executive to see... and what to ignore.

Finding the correct e-mail address of an executive in a large organization of any kind can be difficult. But if you do, your e-mail should mirror almost exactly what you would put in the letter we described above, but be even shorter. The only major difference with sending e-mail is that your subject line is the make or break first thing you need to focus on. The subject line must grab their attention because you must get the e-mail opened if you want to have any chance of it being read. Remember, you are up against an enormous amount of e-mail competition with any executive.

Examples of Attention-Grabbing E-Mail Subject Lines:

- Susan Bishop thinks you'll like this idea (But only if you are really being referred by Susan!)

- Our nonprofit can drive more business into your stores

- Soon KGO TV 7 will be talking about you (Tease that this idea will cause a lot of news)

- Our employees want to help (Insert name of their organization)

- This event broke all records last year (Asking for a sponsorship/ partnership for an event)

You can think of a lot more subject lines, but the important point once again: you must grab your potential partner's attention. Be sure, however, that you don't sound like you are selling anything...or your message will never get opened.

I have put a sample email in the **Resource Center** for your review.

The Introductory Phone Call

Armed with your personal contact's introduction, or with the name, title and telephone number of the person you want to reach, you may feel confident just picking up the phone and calling. However, unless you are experienced at making such over-the-phone (or "cold call") introductions, you run the risk of killing the opportunity before it ever gets off the ground.

I strongly recommend that you start by sending the introductory letter or email. In your letter you can present your thoughts in the most convincing order; you will better position the alignment; you will clearly present the benefits and other key point, and close with a strong call-to-action, all on your terms. It is much, much harder to do this on an introductory "cold" phone call.

Voicemail

If you must make that phone call, be prepared to hear an answering machine. Or in the best of cases, reach the executive's administrative assistant. Ask if you can leave a voicemail for the executive about a business opportunity with your organization. Leaving a message on voicemail is always challenging. You are forced to say a lot in a short amount of time, so you may tend to rush your words, but voicemail offers an excellent opportunity to provide a short, clear, motivating message. Rarely have I heard of people practicing how to leave a good voicemail message, but this is exactly what I recommend. Your message should be no longer than 20-25 seconds and get straight to the point. Here's an example:

Good morning, Thomas. This is Janet Moore, Executive Director of Shelter for the Homeless here in Cleveland. There's a wonderful opportunity to develop a teambuilding event for your employees by having them volunteer on the new homeless shelter we are building. As you know, the press loves to cover this type of community event. I'd like to set up a meeting with you within the next two weeks. I only ask 30 minutes of your time. Please call me at 415-555-1111. Thank you.

Remember to keep it short and provide detail as well as a call-to-action.

Write your message out and practice it several times so that you sound relaxed and clear. Be sure to add a strong benefit that his company will receive by working with you. Most importantly, put excitement in your voice. Your enthusiasm will make him want to return the call. And whatever you say, DO NOT give the impression that you are seeking financial donation. Yes, this may come at some stage of the partnership, but it's too soon now. This call is about offering benefit to their organization, and you don't want to turn them off before they get to know you.

Not Hearing Back Is Not a No…Sometimes

Many times you will not get a response to your letter, e-mail or phone call. This is not necessarily a "no" - executives are just very busy. You now have a good reason to call them directly and ask if they've had a chance to look at your letter or request a meeting. And of course, if you get the administrative assistant, you will be armed with your short pitch. I suggest you use a message similar to the voicemail message above. If you have not been able to reach this executive and/or the administrative assistant to arrange for a meeting after one written message and two follow-up calls, stop… and try to find another door. There is no reason to keep trying to reach a person who is not responding. Go back to your first referral contact, call the human resources department or find another person to help you get inside this organization. Of course, if you were introduced by a mutual contact, see if that person can follow up, after you have tried yourself a few times. If nothing works, move on to the next organization on your priority list.

When You Absolutely Must Send a Proposal or Grant Application

Whether by referral, letter, e-mail or phone call, you have one and only one goal - to get a face-to-face meeting with the executive from your potential partner organization. Remember, you're not trying to get a deal at this stage - you just want to sit down with them. But sometimes you have to send a proposal. I hate when this happens, but it does frequently. And it usually happens when they think you are seeking a donation or other request and they do not understand that you are seeking a more value-driven, longer-term partnership. My best suggestion here is to keep this proposal to the minimum amount of information, whenever possible. Give them enough information to satisfy their questions and be intrigued by the relationship you're proposing, but not enough information for them to say that they're not interested.

If you must send a proposal and are able to write it freely without having to fill in boxes, follow the guidelines in the previous "Send a personal letter" section.

A common practice today, especially when approaching a corporate or independent foundation for a grant, is being required to fill out an application on their website. This can be anywhere from a 10- minute process, to many hours, sometimes even days. These questionnaires will ask very specific information, such as timetables, the proposed program, budgets of your organization, tax ID information, Board members, funding or other areas you are seeking, etc. A few years back I filled out an application for the U.S. government's *Save America's Treasures* grants, and it took me over two weeks to collect the information and write the grant. As I was asking for $750,000, I bit my tongue and filled out all the boxes. Unfortunately, while we made the final round, we didn't win the grant. The good news: such detailed advance proposals are not the general practice.

A proposal should begin with an Executive Summary. This summary should be no longer than 3/4 to 1 page absolute maximum. In many instances, the reader of your proposal (hopefully a high-level executive or program officer) will never need to go past this first page. Lay out everything in those first few paragraphs to convince them that a partnership is in their best interest. Really, this could be your whole proposal, but they will probably want more. The Executive Summary comes at the beginning of your proposal and it is best to write it last, after you have formulated and written down all your other thoughts and added-value benefits. This will let you pick out the key points you want to emphasize in your Executive Summary.

In your proposal, highlight several assets you bring to the partnership. Here are a few suggestions you could mention:

- You have proven experience in programs like this, so the possible partners know they can rely on you. Give an example if possible.

- If you have a well-known brand, emphasize that.

- List Members of your Board who have offered assistance.

- You have an active employee relations/HR department that co-ordinates community volunteer opportunities.

- You have a PR or advertising agency that is already working with you and might be able to help with creative services.

- You have strong relationships with the media in your community.

Unless required, never talk about money in this proposal. This could turn them off, and the numbers may be totally out of whack with what you finally do together. If you are filling out boxes for a grant application, you will be required to put in the amount you're asking for, but in a more open proposal, your focus is on creating an interest in a mutual benefit.

Finally, be sure you put an attention-grabbing cover letter on the proposal. In that letter, focus on two key points: the good alignment between your organizations and what you can bring to their organization.

Jello Job

When searching for potential partners, I suggest you build a database as you collect the information on the people, companies and organizations you research and the organizations that these people/companies support. It's an on-going process to keep such a database up-to-date, but this database will be of exceptional value when looking for future potential partners. This is a great job for an intern, a volunteer or receptionist. It's what I call a "Jello Job" because it can fill in when there are small gaps between other work assignments.

When an arts organization wanted me to look for potential corporate partnerships, I began collecting the program of every cultural or other major event I attended, such as the ballet, symphony, theater, special events and the like. Also, after many fundraising galas or events, nonprofit organizations will place an ad in the local papers thanking their sponsors. I collected these ads and after cross-referencing the companies and organizations that were sponsoring cultural programs and events, I built a database that listed the company and the organizations it supported. Using information-gathering techniques, I filled in the names and contact information for the executives at these organizations. Soon I had a list of well over 200 potential partners I felt would be relevant to our arts organization. It's easy and it works. It's a Jello Job.

Preparing for the First Team Meeting

If you were successful in having an introductory meeting, you are ready to move into a more formal meeting with members of your team and your potential partner's team. To make the best impression and to set the meeting on the most productive course, there are a few essential things that you must do first.

1) Confirm who will be at the team meeting

Confirm with your contact at the potential partner organization who they will be bringing to the team meeting and their positions within the organization.

You want to encourage your potential partner to bring a couple of members of their executive/senior staff and marketing team so that you can get as much top level buy-in of this partnership concept as possible. And try to match the number of people they bring with the number of people you bring. If you are a small organization, you might want to also take a member of your board. And of course you will include your pre-determined "point-person," as s/he will be the primary liaison on all matters concerning the project or campaign and reporting back to the rest of the team.

Note: There's a good chance you're not going to get the CEO or Executive Director of a large company or nonprofit organization at this first team meeting. So I strongly recommend...and this can be a touchy subject...that you don't bring your CEO or Executive Director either, unless you and/or they are a fairly small organization. The reason is this: In such meetings the person at the top of the organization may tend to talk about all the good things your organization is doing.

The focus of this meeting must be on what value your organization can bring to your potential partner. From my experience, this focus on another entity is hard for many leaders. So prepare a follow-up report for your leadership, but if possible, leave them back at the office.

2) Review the research

Review the research you have gathered on this particular organization. Be familiar with its mission statement, any particular projects they are currently developing in their community and the like. As always, you are looking for areas of alignment. Read the bios of the people who will be at the meeting (use LinkedIn, the company website, Facebook, etc.) ahead of time so you and your team will have a better understanding of the person(s) you will be meeting with. Look for areas of commonality between yourself and your organization, such as another organization to which you both belong to or a hobby you share. Mentioning these commonalities during your first meeting may well create a favorable impression and interest.

3) Prepare a list of questions

Prepare a list of questions that were raised during your research and initial idea development. These might include questions about the staff time, funding and/or other services that you may request your partner to provide. Concurrently, prepare answers to such questions about what you bring to the table. In other words, prepare questions you need to have answered, while also preparing for questions you might be asked.

4) Prepare a list of your initial ideas

Prepare a list of your initial ideas and concepts to discuss with this potential partner. For example, if they are building a new homeless shelter, by reviewing what they have done with other organizations and the type of organization they are, you'll have specific ideas of how you might work together. Have your ideas well thought out and based on what you know your team could deliver. Yet remember—the primary objective of this first meeting is to emphasize the value you and your organization can bring to your potential partner's organization. By emphasizing, through your ideas, how you can help their organization, they will be far more likely to be open and enthusiastic about a potential partnership.

5) Avoid a proposal

Do not bring a written formal proposal. At this early point you have no idea if they want a partnership or what type of partnership would work best for all sides. So don't go in with any preconceived notions about what you're going to do.

A Word of Caution

Do not go into this meeting convinced that you have the best idea. The best idea will be the one that you and your partners decide upon together that will best meet your mutual goals. If you come on too strong, too assured, you may quickly alienate your potential partner. However, if you have a strong idea or two that meet the mutual goals, bring these up in an exploratory manner. Talk them out together. Sometimes when you take this softer approach, your partner will show great enthusiasm, even to the point of thinking that it was his or her idea. While it's hard to have someone else take over your idea, your ultimate goal is a strong partnership, so always keep that as your top priority.

Several years back I was involved in a meeting between Wells Fargo Bank and the American Red Cross. I had suggested this meeting to my boss at the Red Cross because I felt there was a wonderful opportunity to develop a mutually rewarding marketing and fund development program. He set the meeting up, and there we were in the impressively large boardroom of Wells Fargo Bank, with its Chief Marketing Officer and a member of her team, along with my boss and me. I had tried to set up a preliminary meeting with my boss to discuss my ideas for an emergency preparedness catalog, with Wells Fargo serving as the sponsoring funder and distributor. However, he felt we should just go to the meeting and see what they wanted to do. So after all the introductions and niceties, there we were, sitting across the table just staring at each other, no one saying a word. Clearly, they thought we had come in with a particular idea in mind. It was embarrassing, for me at least. So I jumped in and introduced the magalog idea I described earlier and explained how I thought it would work for our two organizations.

What we didn't know going into that meeting was that Wells Fargo was just about to launch a new advertising campaign based around the theme "Preparing for Your Financial Future." When their Chief Marketing Officer outlined this campaign, it was amazingly aligned with my idea for an emergency preparedness catalog. Wow! The group seized on the catalog idea. Everyone got excited and added their own thinking. Over the next several months, the idea led to a phenomenally successful and profitable partnership. We were lucky that despite our lack of joint preparation it worked out well. Don't take that chance; be sure to prepare.

Leadership Approval

In spite of the above example, it is imperative that you go into this meeting and all early discussions with the approval of your CEO/Executive Director or senior management. Meet with your leadership and present your thoughts and ideas and get their input and their approval to move forward. It would be a waste of time, embarrassing and potentially damaging to your organization's reputation, to meet with potential partners without this leadership approval.

Where to Meet

If you are a nonprofit organization and have a particular operational program such as a homeless shelter, then offer to have your potential partner tour it, meet your team, and especially meet the people your team and shelter serve. Showing the good work of your organization will create an emotional engagement, and this is an excellent start to a relationship. This goes both ways. Nonprofit organizations always enjoy visiting business operations. A building supply company could offer the homeless shelter partnership team a tour of their warehouse or even of one of the community projects they have worked on in the past. Such on-the-ground visits create an extremely welcoming atmosphere and excitement for your budding partnership.

Suggestions for a Great First Team Meeting

These meetings can take on many different feelings: warm and friendly, welcoming to your organization and the potential of working together. And sometimes they can be somewhat cold and standoffish, with the "other side" taking a "show me what you've got" attitude. Needless to say, I've experienced lots of both.

You want to immediately warm up the room, so I suggest you begin by saying how impressed you've been with this particular organization's commitment to their community. It's important at this beginning point to cite a few examples of this organization's projects or programs that you've seen or at least read about. Start by building them up with true praise and be very careful that it comes across as sincere. The truth is - you may have known very little about this organization until you began your research looking for a potential partner. But now, having read its annual report and other materials from the Internet or their press releases about what they have done in the community, you will be well-prepared to compliment them sincerely. There is no better way to start a meeting and warm up a potentially skeptical audience than to begin with this complimentary approach.

If your friend/contact is accompanying you to this meeting, after all the introductions, have them open the conversation by telling why they felt it was important that your two organizations meet and the value that they think can be gained by both organizations working together. This friend/contact will have the credibility of both potential partners and thus can set the stage perfectly. However, with the stage properly set, this friend/contact should take a backseat to the rest of the conversation for they probably will not be involved in the ongoing relationship.

Following the introductions, the set up and the compliments, talk about the great alignment you see between your two organizations. This is a good point to bring up a particular project or program that you have done in the past, are working on now or that you would like this partnership to consider. This example should be closely aligned with your potential partners' past or current community or cause-related programming. While you are still two separate organizations scrutinizing each other, when you start talking about programs, missions or projects that are closely aligned, the all-important shift will happen in this conversation - you begin moving from they and you...to we.

And what are we going to do about him?

Gorilla in the Room

When bringing together organizations from different sectors, and certainly of different sizes, many times there is a natural uneasiness, the unspoken "gorilla in the room." Bobbi Silten, of the Gap Foundation put it this way: "There's a dynamic that will probably never go away, and that's a power dynamic that's based on money. There's people who hold the cash and the people who need the cash. So in our initial meeting with nonprofits we talk about this power dynamic of money. We say that we can never make that dynamic go away, but what we can do is endeavor to level this power dynamic as much as possible. It's about trust, being transparent and putting the cards on the table."

Once you address this gorilla, sweep it off the table and shoo it out of the room (not always the easiest thing to do!), the difference in organizational size and perceived power imbalances should go away or at least should be diminished to the point of not affecting your working relationship. In most cases, differences will actually benefit the partnership, for each partner is bringing a new perspective and set of experiences and assets to the group.

Openly Describe Your Needs or Challenges

You are seeking a partnership to address a particular program, project, challenge or opportunity for your organization. A for-profit organization may need to raise their company's brand awareness in the community or larger marketplace to drive sales, attract highly qualified employees or for other good reasons. The important point here is to be very clear about what your organization's intentions are - you are seeking this relationship because of specific needs or challenges your organization faces and feel that this potential partner might be well-aligned and motivated to help. Being completely transparent will create an immediate trust and empathy with this potential partner.

For example, if you are a for-profit company, and your objective is to generate sales for your new product or service, don't beat around the bush by saying that you really just want to be a good community citizen (which of course you do), say that your primary objective of this potential partnership is to generate sales. Of course, I might not be that blunt, especially if your idea is to provide a percentage of sales of your product or service to the nonprofit organization. Emphasize that you want to help their organization, but in a manner that would also generate sales for your organization.

If you are a nonprofit organization, and your objective is to find funding to build a homeless shelter, tell them you need to build a homeless shelter and you want their help. Certainly present the important business value proposition of how working with you would provide excellent benefit to their organization - that will best trigger their interest. Just be clear that funding would be necessary to accomplish your goal. When your partner sees that your objective is sincerely to help them meet their goals, they will work hard to meet your goals.

There is nothing that will destroy a partnership faster than being a few steps down the road and finding out that your partner had a hidden agenda, that what they said were their primary goals and objectives at the beginning were not.

> If you want to go fast, go alone. If you want to go farther, go together.
>
> African Proverb

Take Notes

A lot of information, creative ideas, decisions and needs will come flying in this meeting. So it is very important that someone on your team is designated to take detailed notes of the conversation. At the end of this first meeting, an overview of what was discussed, decisions made and next steps should be sent to all parties that are part of the relationship. This is especially important so that people who were not at the meeting, especially your leadership, will be informed with the correct information as soon as possible.

Completing the Exploration Process and Choosing the Right Partner

The next steps depend on what happens at this first team meeting, or you may have held another meeting or two, possibly with some new team members from either organization. At the end of this initial process it's safe to say you're in one of two places:

1) You have mutually agreed that bad timing, poor chemistry, financial restraints, or other such factors preclude you from forming a productive partnership with one or more of your potential partners. It just wasn't the right fit. And so you shake hands, thank each other for their valuable time and move on to your next potential partner.

2) The chemistry was great, the creativity flowed, the financial upside looks great, you've accomplished all that you desired at your meeting(s) and your partnership potential is high. If you have other potential partners, continue on with your other meetings until you and your team are completely assured that you have selected the best partner, and they have selected you.

Having gone through this recommended process, in most cases you will find that one organization stands above all the rest. It has met all or most of your partnership criteria. The project or cause you are addressing together is highly motivational to all of your separate stakeholders, especially your employees. You can't wait to work together.

In rare cases, you'll find that more than one organization fits your partnership criteria. If you are a nonprofit or educational organization, it may be quite possible that you could form a partnership with two or more partners from the for-profit or governmental sectors. However, there needs to be only one nonprofit organizational partner, unless you are supporting a coalition of nonprofits in the same area of interest, such as health issues, homelessness, or other potential nonprofit collaborations. This was the opportunity with the Health and Wellness Fair in Oakland where we had three primary nonprofit and governmental partners, and nearly 90 educational and nonprofit service providers joining together.

Here we are going to assume that you have agreed to move forward with a partnership with your selected cross-sector partner. At this early stage in the partnership development process, several important decisions and elements of your partnership will need to be finalized before moving forward into the actual execution phase. These include:

1) Agreed to pursue working together toward a mutually-reward ing partnership

2) Established a clear understanding of each other's needs and the partnership objectives

3) Explored what each side would bring to the partnership, such as funding, volunteers, services, etc. (Note: You may not have decided on the specifics of what you plan to do but should have a clear understanding of who would be doing what.)

4) Provided assurances that your leadership is supportive of this relationship

5) Agreed, at least initially, to the type of partnership project or

campaign that you want to explore together (new project, fundraising, product endorsement, cause marketing, etc.)

6) Established if there are other partners who should be involved to strengthen the partnership and reach your goals

7) Determined if either party has a public relations or advertising agency (pro bono or paid) that might support this partnership

8) Agreed on a very preliminary timeline

Moving Forward Together

From this point forward there will be many more conversations and meetings. These meetings should be coordinated by the designated point-persons from each partner, and between meetings these point-person should be communicating back and forth on what each side is doing toward their mutual goals. There is no accurate way of estimating how many conversations and meetings will be needed or the amount of time from this point through the completion of your project or campaign. Most projects or cause marketing campaigns require a minimum of six months to properly execute from start to completion, and some require 12 or more months. It all depends on the complexity of the effort you are undertaking together. The key point to remember is that this is not a one-time event, sponsorship or philanthropy relationship. You are developing a long-term partnership with many facets and many benefits for all partners involved. Don't rush this process, there is too much to gain or too much to lose.

Building Trust

Any successful relationship - a marriage, close friendship or a cross-sector partnership - is built upon trust. Nothing forms trust faster than telling the truth and being open and transparent with your potential partner, thus building trust is a huge issue in successful cross-sector partnerships.

Bobbie Silten provided the following example and advice: "At first some nonprofits don't want to show their vulnerability and that may be exactly what they need—to have you help them find what their vulnerabilities are. One of the things that touched me most was how vulnerable our partners were. One organization we had just given a huge increase to told us that they are having real morale issues in their organization and they need our help. I said to the Executive Director, thank you for being so honest. This is what our partnership is about because it said so much to me about how much you trust us and we're going to work together to solve this."

Effective communication is the platform upon which trust and a strong relationship are built. Your communication should be open, honest, and regular. When challenges arise, you must address them immediately, coming from the position of: "What can we do to solve this challenge in such a way that will strengthen the partnership and further our goals?" Your partners, and your own organization, will appreciate your being frank and reacting in a timely way. Indeed, working through such challenges will strengthen the trust among all participants, and prepare you for when future challenges arise.

Transparency

Transparency is a huge issue in the development of successful cross-sector partnerships and especially in cause marketing. Transparency is basically telling the truth - the truth about your organization, your partnership, your goals, which organization is actually receiving the benefit of your cause campaign or project, and how you're raising your money. For example: What exactly is the percentage of donations going to the cause or project? With the rapid growth and success of cause marketing, there has been, most unfortunately, an increase in the number of campaigns that, to be polite, didn't tell the whole truth. For example: saying that "a portion of the proceeds is going to...." is NOT transparent. Is it 10%, 5% or .00001%? The public is not being told the truth. Consequently, the public has become increasingly skeptical about how much money is actually going to the cause, and in some cases, what the cause is in the first place.

Joe Waters provided me with the following example of a campaign that erred on providing transparency. In his post on May 16, 2011, *Urban Outfitters' Cause Marketing* for NPR is a Poor Fit, Joe discusses a cause marketing program between Urban Outfitters and National Public Radio.

Urban Outfitters offered a branded NPR t-shirt on the public radio station's website for $20. Profits from the sales support NPR. However, Urban Outfitters sold the very same branded shirt on its website and a similar version offline in stores for $24, but NPR received no profit from these sales. Joe's concern, as it should be for all of us, is that such practice is "totally confusing for the consumer. If a consumer buys the NPR tee on the Urban Outfitter site, they're probably thinking a portion of the purchase is supporting public radio." Consumers who may have heard the promotional pitch on NPR and then went into an Urban Outfitters' store might feel that the t-shirt they bought in the store was benefiting NPR, when in fact, it wasn't.

There is also the despicable practice of what I call "causeless cause marketing," which is when an advertisement or promotion states that a portion of the proceeds will go to support (fill in the cause here: homelessness, poverty, cancer research, etc.), yet nowhere in the advertisement does it name the specific nonprofit that is the recipient of the funds! To say this is unscrupulous is a wild understatement. When you see one of these faux-cause ads, enjoy the satisfaction of rolling it up into a ball and throwing it in the wastepaper basket.

A recent post on *Causecapitalism.com* highlighted the relationship between transparency and successful business:

"We know that transparency is a strong indicator of a company's social mission. Turns out, it's also good for business. Recently, transparency has been shown to be a significant driver of ultimate financial performance. The thread between transparency and profit is trust. By opening up internal operations, successes and failures to the public and to employees, we demonstrate transparency as a company, which customers like. But the reason customers like this is because it allows them to trust us, to recommend us, to tell us when we err, and to choose us again."

And so we come full circle to the issue of trust. When a company/ nonprofit/cause/campaign is not transparent, it loses our trust, and thus our personal and financial backing. A Cone, Inc. study found the following:

- 91 percent of Americans believe companies should tell them how they are supporting causes, but many do not feel they are getting sufficient information.

- Only 58 percent of Americans believe companies are providing enough details about their cause efforts.

A good example of an organization that requires stringent transparency in all of their cause-related partnerships is the American Red Cross. Here is the required donation language for any cause marketing donation program with the Red Cross:

"XYZ will donate to the American Red Cross, including the amount of the donation as a flat fee (e.g. $1.00 for every shirt sold) or a percentage (e.g. 25% of the retail sales price) and the time frame (e.g. from September 1, 2013 until August 31, 2014)"

This specific donation language is clear and prominently placed on all product packaging and hang tags. The public sees exactly what amount or percentage of their purchase is going to the nonprofit partner, and the timeline of the campaign. This transparency creates trust.

Tim Ogden, Editor-in-chief of *PhilanthropyAction.com*, has proposed a five-part set of standards. While he proposed this rating system specifically for cause marketing campaigns, its guidelines work very well for any cross-sector partnership that has fund development as part of its program. Tim stated, "Any program that doesn't meet all of these standards should be shunned," but then he added, "I know that's not realistic." The five standards are:

1) The program says exactly which charity will receive the funds with enough information for a person to find and investigate the charity on their own.

2) The program says exactly how much money the charity will receive (either in total or from each purchase, with a projection of the total and any minimum or maximums built-in.) Note that percentages, especially such nebulous percentages as "2% of the profits," do not meet this standard. Tell me the money.

3) The program says when the charity will receive the funds.

4) The program says what the funds will be used for or if there are any restrictions on the use of funds. This is especially important when brands link up to very large charities that do lots of things in lots of places (e.g. Save the Children, United Way, World Wildlife Fund). This standard isn't about the good or bad of restricted funds, it's just asking for full disclosure on the terms of the funds and what they will be used for.

5) The program says why the charity was chosen.

Tim said: "I don't expect any program to meet this last standard, but I think it's important to push corporations with charitable programs to use the resources at their disposal to help the general public find good charities. Corporations invest millions of dollars in these cause marketing campaigns. The least they can do is spend some of that money doing due diligence on the charities and telling the public what they find."

Thanks, Tim; excellent guidelines.

Several states are looking closely at the issue of transparency in cause marketing practices, and some have come up with specific recommendations. New York Attorney General Eric Schneiderman released the "Five Best Practices for Transparent Cause Marketing" for both charities and companies engaged in "cause marketing." After reviewing questionnaires sent out to 150 different companies last October, AG Schneiderman concluded that "consumers do not have sufficient information to understand how their purchases will benefit charity." You'll find this report in the **Resource Center** under Legal Considerations for Partnerships.

Maintaining an Efficient and Caring Relationship

As your cross-sector partnership project or campaign progresses, you should be tracking all critical business aspects: Are we on target with our budget; are donations secured or pledged; what's the effectiveness of our public messages, etc.? You should also be tracking the partnership relationship: is it open; is it transparent and trusting; is it working in the best way possible; are we holding each other accountable to the agreements of the partnership?

Here are a few suggestions for developing and maintaining an effective and caring relationship:

1) Keep your focus on the greater good.

There are many bumps along the road in any endeavor, and a cross-sector partnership brings its own unique set of them. Keep your focus on why you are doing this partnership - to beneficially impact the greater good. Nothing overcomes adversity as well as the sincere belief that you are doing the right thing.

2) Keep each other accountable.

Once you have developed your project or campaign plan, keep yourself and each partner accountable for the agreed-upon responsibilities. If one individual or partner organization begins to slide away from their responsibilities, address this issue kindly but immediately. Things happen, circumstances change, people leave organizations. No matter what happens, hold up your end of the bargain and expect the others to do the same. Keep in mind that accountability comes in at all levels. The CEO or Executive Director might have only a few responsibilities that they are being held accountable for during the project or campaign. Your marketing director and/or development director may be held accountable for monthly and even weekly responsibilities. Meanwhile, the point-person for each partner will have on-going, possibly daily activities and multiple areas for which they are accountable.

3) Communicate!

Without clear, constant and caring communication, any relationship is doomed to fail. The point-person from each organization bears responsibility to keep their organization and its stakeholders fully informed of all aspects of the partnership, good and not so good. Keep and publish minutes of your meetings, set regular times to convene as a full partnership team, and when serious issues, disagreements or other challenges arise (and they will), communicate your concerns and work them out as a team as soon as possible.

4) Be open and flexible to new ideas and new opportunities.

New ideas and new opportunities frequently arise in cross-sector partnerships. A new partner may wish to join your partnership who could add to your overall success. A special event may be offered, a major media interview requested, or an entirely off-the-wall but exciting idea presented. As long as these new opportunities are "on-strategy," explore their potential, while keeping in mind your resources and priorities.

5) Deal with a problem.

If one of your partners/organizations becomes too set in their ways, inflexible to new opportunities or is creating tension among the other partners, address the situation immediately before it sours the entire partnership. In the worst case scenario, the problem person/organization needs to leave the partnership.

6) Have fun!!

Partnerships are like any project: they're a lot of work. Once in a while you just need to let off some steam. Go out for a beer together, meet for a barbecue in someone's backyard, have a semi-competitive game of miniature golf... anything where laughter rules over work.

The Ultimate Goal

The ultimate goal of a good cross-sector partnership is not just the accomplishment of the first project, program or campaign. The ultimate goal is that you establish multiple linkages between your organizations and that over the years your relationship becomes indispensable to each other. After all is said and done, what makes the partnership successful, is that you came together to create not just benefit for yourselves and your organization, but as importantly, to generate good for your community and society as a whole. And for the for-profit partner, you are starting to make your organization glow.

Project or Campaign Concepts

During your individual assessment processes, and together as a team in your initial partnership meetings, you have begun discussing what type of project or campaign you want to undertake. There are an endless number of projects or campaigns that a partnership can undertake. But you have to come together with well-defined objectives.

What Has Been Done Before?

In many cases, you don't have to invent a project or campaign totally from scratch. My recommendation is that you search the Internet for organizations, projects or campaigns that have involved your general area of focus. If your campaign is not in competition with a similar existing project, the people who have designed, managed or directed the project will often gladly give you the details, challenges, and success stories of what they did. They will share ideas, their corporate partners and any cross-sector partnerships (or the project will be described on their website) and possibly even their specific architectural plans, budgets and other very usable material for your project. This research of other project experiences is also critically important to find out where something went wrong, where an obstacle came up that could have derailed their plans and how they overcame or did not overcome this obstacle. Once you have followed this simple research approach and narrowed down your list to those projects or organizations that you feel are most closely aligned with what your team has in mind, reach out and contact these folks!

Ask these questions and follow the answers:

- What's been done before?
- By whom?
- How did they raise their funding?
- What were the results?
- How did they measure their results?
- What were their challenges?
- Would they provide you with detailed information on their project/campaign?
- Could you collaborate with this organization to share results and on-going information?

People and organizations are proud of what they were able to accomplish and they will be willing to share with you, in almost all cases, what they have done.

So now is the time to fine-tune your ideas and select the type and scope of your project or campaign. While there is a lot of excitement at this stage, be careful not to take on too much. Be very specific about what you plan to do and carefully weigh your objectives with the partnership's ability to meet those objectives. It's much better to start small and build upon your success than to try to change the world and change little to nothing.

Once you have selected your project or campaign area of focus, communicate this selection to all of your stakeholders to start generating excitement and buy-in. And of course, secure the all-important approvals by the leadership of each partner team.

Now your partnership will seem very real, very doable, because you have vocalized and visualized what you will do together. You have set your sights on the center of the target, and as you will find, the universe will turn toward you and help, because this project or campaign is larger than yourselves - it will benefit the greater good. This quote by Goethe that has been on my wall since I was a young man says it all:

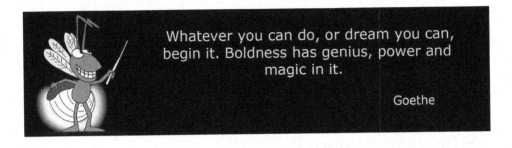

Whatever you can do, or dream you can, begin it. Boldness has genius, power and magic in it.

Goethe

Negotiation/Legal/Agreements
Internal Agreement

Undoubtedly your organization's team and leadership will have met to discuss the selected project or campaign and have discussed the overall scope and flow of your organization's involvement. There will need to be a Written Agreement between the two or more partner organizations, which we will explore later in this section. What is most important at this point is for each individual organization to assess their role, the scope of their involvement, financial expectations and limitations, finalize the internal partnership team and clarify any and all concerns that need to be well-understood and finalized before you begin the development of a formal Written Agreement with your partners. Indeed, as you move through your internal discussions, it is a very good idea to begin compiling a detailed list of everything that you feel should be included in the Written Agreement.

Internal Approval Process

As emphasized earlier, having your CEO, Executive Director, and/or leadership team fully behind and supportive of your partnership is an absolute necessity before going into the finalization of your partnership. Also, one of your key internal agreements is having an approval process in place before you finalize the Written Agreement of the partnership. This will make your communications and activities with your partners move much more swiftly. You should explain to your partners in your preliminary meetings that you've (hopefully) already established a smooth internal approval process for the partnership. This not only communicates your professionalism but also that you have set up your internal systems to support this partnership.

Internal Budgets and Timeline

Part of your internal agreement will be key decisions concerning what financial support your organization is willing to provide, in both cash and in-kind donations. Also determine to your best estimate the amount of staff and/or volunteer time, and the use and cost of using outside public relations, advertising or graphics agencies, and any and all other personnel and/or supplies that will affect your organization's internal cost for this partnership. While you will not have final partnership project or campaign cost estimates at this early juncture, you need to know what your organization is willing to spend before finalizing the partnership. Much of this information may have been established in your internal Assessment Process. However, now that you have a much clearer idea of your potential partnership project or campaign, you should reassess this very critical area of budgets.

As with your preliminary internal budgets, you should start estimating the amount of time you will allocate to your staff and other resources. These will not be firm estimates at this early juncture due to the need for your final partnership Written Agreement and just the normal give-and-take of a project or campaign's development. However, it's wise not to underestimate the time it will take to manage and execute a six to 12 month campaign.

Negotiation Techniques

When bringing together parties and partners from different sectors, with different backgrounds, sometimes with very different business systems or philosophical approaches, you may help need to find common ground in developing your partnership. The seminal work in negotiations was *The Harvard Negotiation Project*. Based on this research, Roger Fisher and William Ury wrote the best-selling book, *Getting to Yes, Negotiating Agreement Without Giving In*. With the review and approval of William Ury, I've taken some thoughts and suggestions from their work which I think will be helpful to smooth the path and avoid the pitfalls that can happen when different parties, especially from different sectors, are coming together to develop a working relationship, leading to a mutually beneficial Written Agreement.

While the premise of this book is focused on achieving the greatest amount of organizational benefit by seeking mutual success and focusing on the greater good, it would be naïve to think that individuals and organizations enter into a partnership only to help the other side or only to help the greater good. We explore partnerships to gain advantage for our own business objectives. And this is good, for this perspective motivates us to seek the greatest amount of benefit.

In *Getting to Yes* (GTY), the authors discuss this all-so-human aspect of negotiations. "People get angry, depressed, fearful, hostile, frustrated, and offended. The egos are easily threatened, they see the world from their own personal vantage point, and they frequently confuse perceptions with reality." The authors emphasize, "Failing to deal with others sensitively as human beings prone to human reactions can be disastrous for a negotiation." This concern applies to all people-to-people interactions: in a personal relationship, in a legal confrontation and in a more compassionate agreement to provide building materials and supplies for a new homeless shelter. In all these relationships it is important to maintain a good working relationship. As the GTY authors say, "Base the relationship on accurate perceptions, clear communication, appropriate emotions, and a forward-looking, purposive outlook." The following is a list of observations and suggestions taken from GTY that will help you in your discussions to find common ground throughout your partnership and people relationships:

- Recognize and understand emotions, theirs and yours. Look for the underlying "why" that is creating these emotions.

- Allow both sides to let off some steam when necessary. The best strategy to adopt while the other side lets off steam is to listen quietly without responding to their attacks. Give the speaker every encouragement to speak himself out, and leave little or no residue to fester.

- If you are not hearing what the other side is saying there is no communication.

- Understanding is not agreeing. Unless you convince them that you do grasp how they see it, you may be unable to explain your viewpoint to them.

- It is clearly unpersuasive to blame the other party for the problem, to engage in name-calling, or to raise your voice.

- You can improve communication by limiting the size of the group meeting.

- The basic problem in a negotiation lies not in conflicting positions, but in the conflict between each side's needs, desires, concerns, and fears.

- Make a list to sort out the various interests of each side. It helps you to write them down as they occur to you.

- If you want to make the other side appreciate your interests, begin by demonstrating that you appreciate theirs.

- In a negotiation, you want to know where you are going, and yet be open to fresh ideas.

- By looking from the onset for the single best answer, you're likely to short-circuit a wiser decision-making process in which you select from a large number of possible answers.

- Place yourself firmly in the shoes of the other person - you'll understand his/her problem and what kind of options might solve it.

- It makes sense to draft possible terms of an agreement as you go. Working on a draft helps to keep discussions focused, tends to surface important issues that might otherwise be overlooked, and gives a sense of progress.

- Before you even begin to negotiate, it makes sense to envision what a successful agreement might look like. Think about what it might take to persuade the other side - and you - to accept a proposed agreement, rather than continuing to negotiate.

In the end, it may be that you are not able to reach agreement. In such cases a successful negotiation is one in which you and they amicably and effectively discover that the best way to advance your respective interests is for each of you to look elsewhere and not try further to reach agreement.

There was one paragraph in *Getting to Yes* that struck to the core of creating understanding and moving forward together: "There is power in developing a good working relationship between the people negotiating. If you understand the other side and they understand you; if emotions are acknowledged and people are treated with respect even when they disagree; if there is clear, two-way communication with good listening; and if people problems are dealt with directly, not by demanding or offering concessions on substance, negotiations are likely to be smoother and more successful for both parties." Amen.

Legal Issues

Due to the rapid growth of cross-sector partnerships and cause marketing campaigns, and the fact that the majority of cause marketing campaigns include some form of charitable donation/ public financial relationship, there is increasing focus on legal issues and requirements. A term that is often used concerning this cross-sector relationship is "commercial co- venture." This scrutiny is good for partnership endeavors as a whole, especially in light of some campaigns that have been less than transparent in their claims or their actual donations to nonprofit causes.

As part of your Written Agreement you will need to include or at least be aware of where your project or campaign may need compliance with any local or state laws. The need for a Written Agreement, which can be as binding as a legal contract, varies considerably depending on the proposed activity your project or campaign is undertaking. For example, if your child is going door-to-door collecting donations for UNICEF, there is no need for a contract between your child and your neighbor. However, if you are developing a charitable sales promotion where one dollar from every purchase of a product goes to a particular charity, the recommended best practice is for the business to have a written contract when it conducts a promotional program invoking the name of the charity.

Thankfully, we have some help. Ed Chansky is an attorney with the Las Vegas Office of Greenberg Traurig LLP. He is a trusted advisor to many national advertisers and nonprofit organizations in the field of cause-related marketing, charitable promotions, sweepstakes, contests, rebates, coupons, and e-commerce.

Ed offers this general advice:

- Always document the agreement between the nonprofit and for-profit entities in a charitable or cause-related promotion.

- Do not use the name of the charity in your solicitation without a written agreement.

- Specific campaigns, such as charitable sales promotions, may trigger the need to register with your state, and sometimes be bonded by the state, where such laws apply.

The regulations covering charitable promotions, cause marketing and any cross-sector campaign that involve financial solicitation vary greatly from state to state. And a local cross-sector partnership is under the same regulations as a national campaign. It's always advisable for your corporate counsel or the lawyer on your nonprofit's board of directors to review this Written Agreement and see if there might be need for a more formal contract.

Ed Chansky has provided a *Cause Marketing Compliance Checklist* for this book which can be found in the **Resource Center** under *Legal Considerations for Partnerships*. Ed also provided an article entitled: *For Goodness Sake: Legal Regulation and Best Practices in the Field of Cause-Related Marketing*, which can also be found in the **Resource Center**.

Written Agreement

Wise partnerships develop and approve a Written Agreement among all participating partners prior to moving into the implementation phase of your partnership. This agreement step is not to be overlooked, no matter what the size of your partnership. Practically speaking, much may change between the time of this Written Agreement and the completion of your campaign. New factors will come up, new opportunities may arise, you may find that there is a new partner that would add a lot to what you are trying to accomplish, and so you add them to the partnership, and you will need to amend your original Written Agreement.

This Written Agreement is critically important because it sets the parameters of what the partnership wishes to accomplish and who is obligated to do what. As Ed Chansky emphasized: "A legal contract may be necessary if you are requiring particular payment amounts, developing a product licensing contract and possibly for the use of logos and other necessities."

The actual writing of the Written Agreement can be undertaken by any of the partners - whomever the partnership feels can best develop the first and subsequent drafts.

Your Written Agreement should include at least the following:

1) Who are the partners involved, what are their principal roles and what is the overall management structure of the partnership?

2) Why are you doing this? What is the problem you are trying to solve or effort you want to accomplish together?

3) What are you actually going to do? Is it a specific project, a fundraising campaign, a new product introduction with a donation aspect? Be specific in describing what you're going to do.

4) What personnel from each partner will be involved, with what specific tasks, reporting to whom within the partnership's management structure?

5) Is there a split of profits, royalty payments or charitable donation as part of your campaign? Define the arrangement. If there is a total donation/payment commitment, define the amount and when is this payment/commitment due to the nonprofit. Any financial arrangement must be spelled out explicitly in your Written Agreement. Nothing can get in the way of a good relationship as quickly as disagreements over money.

6) Where will this project/campaign take place: in your city, on a regional or national level, in-store, online, etc.?

7) When are you going to execute this campaign? Provide a detailed timetable from beginning through the estimated completion of the campaign/project/program.

8) What is your preliminary project or campaign budget? How much money is it going to take to accomplish your goals, and factor in not just cash but also staff time and overhead?

9) Who is paying for what? Be very specific as to who's putting up what amounts of money or in-kind supplies or other tangible and intangible assets. It would be wise to develop a preliminary campaign/program budget.

10) Will additional PR or advertising agencies or other external services/personnel be utilized for the campaign? Be specific as to who is providing the services and who is paying for the services. This would also include the involvement of volunteers from the partner organizations. What would be their role, how many hours would you estimate they would be dedicating to this particular program, etc.?

11) How will you measure the success of the campaign? What metrics will you use to measure, such as increased sales, money raised, products sold, publicity garnered, volunteers attracted and other goals of your partnership? This area of measurement and setting up metrics at the beginning of your campaign is highly important so that you will be able to analyze the effort versus the reward at the end of the project's first year or campaign.

This Written Agreement provides a blueprint of accountability. Things change, people and their situations change, and sometimes a partner will not hold up their end of the agreement. This Written Agreement will provide an independent reminder of the allocation of responsibilities.

When Money Is Involved, Who Gets What?

In most cross-sector partnerships and cause marketing endeavors, there is usually one primary beneficiary. However, sometimes the financial beneficiaries are not so clearly defined. If a donation to a particular cause results from the sale of a product or service, then both the nonprofit and for-profit are financially benefiting. A good model of such a multiple beneficiary partnership was the cause marketing campaign described earlier with Campbell's Soup, Kroger Stores, and the Susan G. Komen Race for the Cure. Campbell's profited from the soup sales, as did the Kroger stores, and Susan G. Komen received donations from each can of soup sold. In this type of partnership, you must clearly define the amount of money going to the nonprofit from each product sold. However, you usually will not stipulate how much money either Campbell's or Kroger's made from their sales of soup. Few for-profit organizations would provide that inside margin/profit information. The nonprofit should negotiate its best donation/benefit possible but not push for internal information from the for-profit partner(s).

The situation is quite different if there are two nonprofits or other partners from the same sector who will both benefit financially from the donations of a particular campaign or program. For example, if a nonprofit organization which runs a homeless shelter teams together with a nonprofit food bank to develop a community-wide fundraising program for their mutual benefit, there would need to be an upfront, agreed-upon split of the donations received from the effort. In these mutually beneficial campaigns, I always emphasize the importance of pooling all of your resources and splitting the final revenue from the campaign/program 50-50. This way everyone is working together for mutual benefit, and no one has an advantage over the other. The only exceptions would be if one partner does much more work or underwrites much more of the expenses.

The Signing

OK, maybe I'm a bit dramatic but I feel that after all the discussions, chosen project, final plans, negotiations, legal review (if necessary) and the Written Agreement is ready to sign...you should celebrate! Well, sign first, then celebrate. Of course, you can mail the agreement back and forth, but what's the fun in that? Don't miss this opportunity to get the full partnership teams together, bring in a pizza or two, (root) beer, and start this amazing journey together on a high note. You are about to do something very special.

Moving Forward Together

Congratulations; you have a partnership! Your Written Agreement is signed, and all parties are excitedly moving forward toward their primary objectives and jointly-held ultimate goals. Your Written Agreement has provided a detailed confirmation of the type of project or campaign that the partners are undertaking together. You have addressed not only what you are going to do but who is responsible for the various tasks to be undertaken. As every cross-sector partnership program, project and cause marketing campaign is different in type, size, scope, geographical location, target audiences, partner configuration, funding requirements, and so many more factors and variables, there is really no way to provide here step-by-step guidelines through the entire start-to-completion development process to cover all potential situations. However, I trust with what I provide in this guidebook you will have a very full toolkit of information and support materials to develop your own blueprint to implement a highly successful project or campaign.

Strategy Development

You might have the greatest cause, the most desperate need, but if it is communicated or positioned poorly, if it doesn't hit the emotional buttons that make people pull out their wallets, volunteer their time, or tell their friends, your campaign is doomed to fail. To motivate people, you need a marketing strategy.

Your marketing strategy is a plan-of-action designed to achieve a particular goal. It's asking your team the question: "How are we going to motivate our audiences to do what we want them to do?". It's been said that a strategy must be the most carefully crafted set of words for your organization. And this is true, because when you have finally set your strategy, each tactic, each event, each message or project of your campaign must be "on-strategy"...and if it's not, don't do it. Anything that pulls you off strategy will certainly frustrate the partners, waste a lot of time, money and effort, and potentially throw your entire project or campaign off its primary mission.

There are two basic elements to your strategy:

- Your creative strategy

- Your tactical strategy

Creative Strategy

Developing creative strategy is the really fun part of a campaign. This is where you are thinking up the ideas, messages, campaign slogans and creative techniques that you feel will best communicate your campaign to your target audiences. It's fun, yes, but it's based entirely on:

- Determining exactly what your partnership aims to accomplish. What is the cause, what is the need, what can you realistically do to create change for the better?

- Limiting your effort to a specific project or goal that can be accomplished. Do not try to fix the homeless problem in the United States; rather, build a homeless shelter in your community. That you can do.

- Having a clear understanding of the competitive landscape. How are other organizations or campaigns addressing the same or similar issues? Your creative strategy must set you apart from any potential competition

- Identifying and understanding the various audiences to whom you want your campaign messaging delivered. If you don't have a clear understanding of your target audiences, you can accomplish this through surveys and market research. You do not need to reach everyone, but you must reach those who can influence, donate, or participate in your cause endeavor.

- Designing your message(s) so that your audiences understand the problem, believe in the solution you are proposing, and ideally, why this is important to them personally. If you can create a relationship, or at least empathy, between the problem and your audience, your potential for success is greatly increased.

- Developing your "call-to-action." What do you want your audiences to actually do? Without a strong call-to-action, the audiences you reach may be better educated about your cause, but they may not be motivated to help you.

- Determining the style and tone of your campaign. Will your campaign messaging be highly emotional or will you use guerrilla marketing tactics or a more straightforward and informational appeal?

This last area of style and tone is of particular importance. All campaigns have or should have a distinct style and tone. We have all seen those advertisements or public service announcements of starving children with tears in their eyes holding out an empty bowl for food. This is the gut wrenching "I'm starving and I need your help," emotional campaign. The photos are dramatic; the announcer's voice is pleading: the call-to-action is urgent; the inference is clear: if you don't help me now, I may die.

Creativity Trumps Clutter

It is immensely challenging to cut through all the clutter and information that the general public and the media receive on a daily basis. If your business or organization can provide something that is highly creative, that stands out from the rest, and if possible, provides humor... this will create attention. Though remember, it is essential that your creativity stays focused on the strategy of your project or campaign.

Hold nothing back on the creativity of your ideas. The crazier, more off-the-wall ideas the better, for they just might work, or at least they will stimulate the more practical ideas. One campaign I designed involved asking Bay Area residents if they could "Survive the Tidal Wave" that was going to hit (a very inland) Santa Clara, California. The "Tidal Wave" was the name of a new looping roller coaster at Marriott's Great America. We even sent out a Tidal Wave "survival kit" to all Bay Area media outlets, which included a lucky rabbit's foot, chocolate bar, a compass, and an invitation to the ride's opening, all wrapped-up within a professionally-prepared first aid kit. This crazy idea was so successful that the media not only provided tremendous coverage of the ride's opening but actually wrote about the survival kit itself in their stories!

Or there was the time we put huge running shoes and an enormous race number chest tag on an African elephant to promote the annual *Examiner's Bay to Breakers* foot race, which provided benefit to several nonprofit organizations.

Photo by Bruce Burtch

We sent a press release to the media stating that "the world's greatest runner" was going to participate in the race and called a press conference. Little did they know how "great" the runner was until they came to the press conference!

Of all the different styles and tones a campaign can utilize, using humor is probably the most challenging. As when telling a joke, the punch-line must work and not turn your audience off. Many campaigns take the more traditional approach of delivering a straight message - not too emotional and certainly not humorous, in their appeal for your participation or donation. Most health issue campaigns, such as those for cancer research, tend to communicate the seriousness of the need or provide a warm, fuzzy feeling, such as sending children with cancer to a summer camp, without tears or humor but with lots of emotion.

More and more, you are seeing special event and public presentation campaigns that are not necessarily supported by media advertising or public service announcements. Pledge walks, foot races and other physically active events are designed to attract participants and pledges for their participation. The event is the campaign, though there is a tremendous amount of promotion work to attract the participants and the pledges. The Internet and social media are also allowing for new types of events. The "flash mob" is another example. In most cases, these are just done for fun or entertainment, but increasingly as a guerrilla marketing technique.

My personal favorite marketing technique is this in-your-face, guerrilla marketing approach to grab the attention of the public and create an instant and strongly favorable reaction to whatever cause is being promoted. In most cases, these "shock and awe" approaches are designed specifically to attract immediate media coverage because of their outrageousness or as I prefer to think, their creativity!

To leverage the marketing impact, whenever possible I design campaigns to bring together a combination of creative elements spread over a multiple-month period. This combining of creative elements is by far the most effective technique to get the maximum bang for your usually limited buck. Whichever way you develop your creative strategy and the supporting style and tone of your campaign, I recommend that you present the problem you're trying to address as dramatically as possible and directly connect that problem to how your solution is going to solve or at least have a beneficial effect on the problem. By all means, focus on the emotion of your appeal. Emotion sticks; emotion drives response. Making the problem real for the audience and touching their heartstrings is powerful. However, remember there is a fine line between an emotional appeal and one that is over the top and sometimes degrading to those you are portraying. A good example of this understanding of where to draw the line is the policy of the American Red Cross for their publicity photos or public service announcements. In Red Cross messaging you will never see a child crying or begging for help. They feel that such an approach demeans the plight of the disaster victims and the seriousness of the situation. They have communicated the emotional need to support victims of disaster, natural or otherwise, quite successfully without resorting to tearful pleas.

Because most cause-related campaigns do not have the advertising budgets of a nationally-marketed consumer product, or any advertising budget at all, they will be relying entirely on free public service announcements, editorial coverage, PR, special events and other efforts that are not costly. If your campaign budget is modest or low, your creative strategy and ultimate messaging to the public must have strong impact if it is to stand out among the thousands of messages that bombard the public daily.

All fun aside, even when you want to support your partner's ideas, or your own ideas, sometimes an idea is just not right for the campaign. Trying to be humorous about a serious disease or social problem could have devastating repercussions. Or not clearly thinking through the message that a particular photograph or story might convey to the public, could bring about the exact opposite reaction you were seeking to create. In your brainstorming sessions, put every idea up on the wall. Then choose the one(s) that best conveys the messages you wish to promote, in the most creative way, without in any way causing damage to your brand or campaign.

A tip: People support what they create. Listen well in these meetings for the good ideas of your potential partner and/or their agencies. When they bring up an idea, explore it and see if it could fit nicely into the program you're discussing. If it does… they will support it.

The rule of thumb I have always used is that the smaller your budget is, the more creative and impactful your message must be.

Don't Rush the Process

The development of your creative strategy cannot be accomplished in one or two meetings. As this is probably the most important part of your entire project or campaign development, you do not want to rush this process. You may have predetermined that the creative strategy will be initially designed by a subcommittee of the partnership team, ideally those with marketing, public relations, or other creative talents and experience. And of course, now is when you get your pro bono advertising or public relations agencies involved. Though if your partnership is a relatively small team, then the entire team might undertake the development of your creative strategy.

In any case, the development pace of your creative strategy will be determined greatly by the information that you have on hand or have found about the project, cause, the audiences and other factors outlined above. The development of the key points of your campaign messaging, call-to-action, slogans and/or other communications should be developed as the final part of this creative development strategy. So don't jump into the fun stuff first. Your final messaging must be based on real information.

Having been involved in innumerable cause projects and campaign strategy development efforts, I know there really is no exact science on how to develop your overall creative strategy. As in any science or in baking a cake, you start with the basic elements, stir them together and go from there.

Slogans as Part of Your Creative Strategy

Your project or campaign will rarely need a separate logo. Indeed, in almost all cases you want to use the more established logos of your partners to lend credibility to your partnership effort. However, campaign names and slogans can be important when well-conceived and executed, for they can galvanize attention to your cause. They should be short, easily remembered, and communicate what the partnership effort is all about. For the 5th Annual Health and Wellness Fair in Oakland we developed the slogan: *Your Road to Wellness*. It communicated clearly that by coming to our Health Fair you were on the road to better health.

Tactical Strategy

Once you have determined your creative messages and strategy, you move on to the development of your tactical (sometimes called operational) strategy, which is how you deliver your creative strategy to your target audiences. Your tactical strategy will involve many elements:

- Determine the priority of the audiences you wish to reach in your campaign. Your creative strategy has defined who your strategic audiences are. Now you want to list them in order of importance. If you have limited funding or team bandwidth to reach them all, focus on your top priority audiences first.

- If your creative strategy suggests different messages to different audiences (sometimes a very smart tactic, as long as they are dead-on with your creative strategy) or a particular order in which your campaign messages should be delivered, determine the best order and audience targets for your messaging.

- Is the campaign being rolled out in different phases? For example, will you need to complete a fundraising campaign before you start construction of your homeless shelter or other project?

- If you have an advertising, PR, or promotional budget, what media will be your primary and secondary delivery mechanisms (print, radio and TV, social media, online, etc.)?

- How you are allocating your budget and staff time to the different areas of media, creative and materials development, roll-out phases of the campaign and other cost and time elements?

- Who will be managing and how will they be held accountable for each part of the campaign?

Operational Timeline

With all the pieces of your tactical strategy defined, now is the time to develop a master operational calendar or timeline. This timeline should include not only all of the many elements of your creative and tactical strategies; it should also include who will be responsible for managing each element. When developing such a detailed timeline, be sure to take into account any holidays, major events, such as annual community or professional sports activities, which might possibly conflict with your obtaining maximum media and public exposure. Many cities have a listing of the events and activities of their primary nonprofit organizations. For example, San Francisco's *Nob Hill Gazette* weekly newspaper publishes a listing of all major society events. You do not want to schedule your project or campaign's press conference or other significant activity and find it competes directly with another potentially larger media or public interest-generating program or holiday event.

Once finalized, this operational timeline guides all of your partnership's plans, decisions, your funding requirements, everything in the execution of your project or campaign. Do not overlook the importance of establishing and following this critical timeline.

Creative Development and Problem Solving

There may be several times throughout your cross-sector partnership development process when you will need to address a problem or develop a new creative approach, especially when attempting to identify potential partners, determining the desired project or cause campaign or when developing your creative and tactical marketing strategies. At such times you may wish to hold what is commonly called a "brainstorming session." These sessions have varying degrees of success because the discussions tend to flow in many directions, and naturally, people with the strongest belief that their own idea is the best will usually try to convince others to follow their path.

There is a much better way to approach this need to find a solution or better idea - by having the sessions and feedback of ideas structured in such a way that everyone has equal input and especially, moving the process from individual positions to group thinking.

Bob Lanier is CEO of BioClaris, a company which teaches how to directly access specific brain systems associated with generating ideas. They have developed the Bioclaris® Method for creative development and problem solving. It is, quite simply, the most effective approach to obtaining the maximum results from group thinking I have ever seen, and it's fun. Bob has kindly provided to this book, and more importantly to you the reader, their unique step-by-step approach to achieving the optimum results for creative development and problem-solving.

I highly recommend this process as a powerful teambuilding, problem-solving and idea-generating opportunity to maximize your effectiveness in conceiving and developing your project or cause marketing campaign. You'll find the Bioclaris® Method in the **Resource Center** under Creative Development and Problem Solving, along with more detailed information, including templates to help you manage the process. The Bioclaris® Method is a gift to us all in our collective desire to make our organizations more effective and to best tap the creative juices of our team and partners.

Marketing Plan

You've heard the expression, "If you don't know where you are going, then any path will take you there." The point of this expression to me is that sometimes people and organizations will grab onto a good idea and start executing it immediately, without stepping back and taking the time to develop a fully thought-out Marketing Plan. This is a huge mistake because rarely, if ever, will this approach meet your partnership objectives. Your Marketing Plan must identify all the opportunities to communicate and promote the partnership to all your stakeholder audiences, and this plan must provide a step-by-step process to achieve your objective(s).

First and foremost, your Marketing Plan is based on your creative and tactical strategies. As you develop the many areas of your Marketing Plan, some of the elements of your tactical strategy may change, and this may also affect your overall timetable. In most cases, these course corrections are based on new ideas and new opportunities and thus are good for the overall effort. However, rarely, if ever, should you change your creative strategy. Your creative strategy is the solid rock upon which all of your messaging, marketing and motivation is built. And as I emphasized earlier, if something comes up that is not on strategy - don't do it.

The Marketing Wheel

A large amount of opportunities and approaches can be incorporated into a Marketing Plan. The following diagram is what I, and probably many others, call "The Marketing Wheel." Think of it as a creative work in progress. You start by putting your project or cause campaign in the middle, and you surround it with all the different marketing disciplines you might possibly integrate into this campaign. These include public relations, media relations, social media, special events, speaking engagements, internal and external communications, printed materials and other marketing activities.

At this early stage, don't let the large amount of opportunities on this Marketing Wheel overwhelm you. In fact, you should be excited to see all that you and your team might be able to accomplish. As you develop your campaign in more detail, you may add some areas or possibly take some off your Marketing Wheel, depending on time, money, volunteers and staff requirements. Working together, your team will decide which opportunities on the Marketing Wheel have the highest priority and the highest potential for success.

As you can see by this depiction of the Marketing Wheel, there are many areas of marketing and promotional opportunities for your project or cause. And each of these areas of opportunity may have several subcategories. For example:

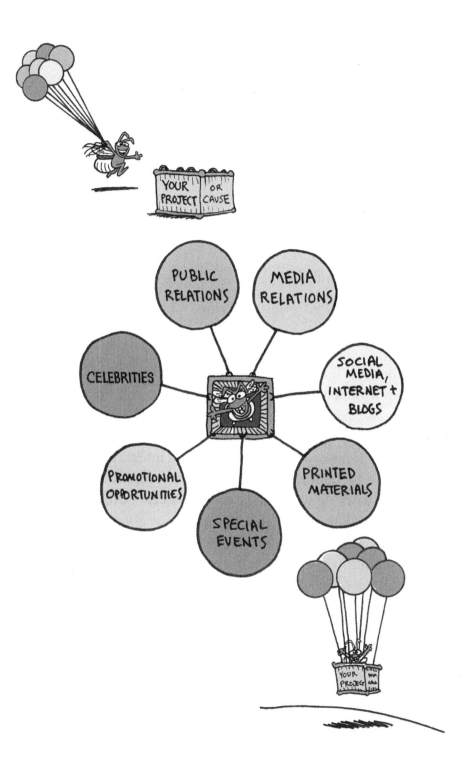

Printed Materials

- brochures and flyers

- newsletters

- direct mail

- posters

- pinups and plaques

Promotional Opportunities

- in-store displays

- milk cartons and shopping bags

- movie theater PSA slides and video

- cooperative promotions

Unfortunately, many marketing plans do not explore all of the opportunities available, not because they aren't important but because sometimes the partners don't even think about them. And that's a great opportunity lost. I find it very useful to use this diagram to make sure that I'm not missing an opportunity to integrate into the Marketing Plan. And I look for others that I may not have thought about. For example, by working with a local grocery store, United Markets, I was able to put a public service announcement for a Red Cross emergency preparedness project on tens of thousands of their shopping bags that were passed out in their stores for a one month period. We also developed a four-color slide of the same public service announcement (PSA) and had the slide projected in San Francisco Bay Area movie theaters. Both of these marketing opportunities were produced at very little cost, the placements were provided for free and they reached an untold number of people when they unpacked their grocery bags or waited to watch the movie. And did I mention...all for free?

The complete development of your Marketing Plan and its implementation may be the most detailed and time-consuming aspect of your project or cause campaign. But it is the Marketing Plan that drives the funding and promotional success of your project or cause, and it can be really fun to execute.

The goal of your Marketing Plan is to develop a step-by-step action plan and a blueprint that guides all aspects of your creative and tactical strategy. Each and every aspect of your Marketing Plan must be directed by the strategy of the campaign (which we detail in the next section) and must reinforce your messages and be consistent throughout the campaign.

Gather your partnership team, or a marketing subcommittee of the larger partnership team, and explore each of the individual opportunities around this Marketing Wheel. For each different marketing discipline/opportunity, ask these questions:

1) What elements fall under each category around the Marketing Wheel?

2) Who on our team has experience in working in this particular area?

3) How can we take our overall creative strategy and apply it to this particular area?

4) What can we do to maximize our campaign's exposure through this area? Be specific.

5) If we don't have the expertise internally to address this particular area, who might we enlist to help us?

Before you actually execute each area of the Marketing Wheel, you will need to have finalized your campaign's creative strategy, any slogans and key messaging statements. However, at this point you are just making a laundry list of all the different areas and subcategories of your marketing opportunities.

Media Relations

To emphasize the large amount of opportunities, let's dive into one of the circles of the Marketing Wheel - media relations. Here is a list of the significant amount of potential opportunities which fall under the Media Relations aspect of your project or cause campaign, and there may be more.

- Press conferences

- Press releases

- Public Service Announcements (PSAs)

- Photography

- Video, audio and YouTube releases

- Content research and development

- Media training for company spokespersons

- Media list development

- Radio and TV talk show appearances

- Interviews with newspapers, magazines, Internet and blog reporters

- Media contests and promotions

- Translation of media materials into different languages

- Media associations

The use of social media might also fall under the Media Relations category, as you are using social media to communicate your messages out to different audiences. However, we will address that area separately.

I put Media Relations at the top of the Marketing Wheel because it is that important to your project or campaign. No other area of the Marketing Wheel or the overall fund development or promotional campaign provides as much reach and impact to the largest amount of people, in the most efficient way, than a well-conceived and well-executed media relations program. If you have a good story to tell, and you do, there is a terrific amount of opportunity to share this story through the media to the public. Every opportunity in the category of Media Relations can be provided to your organization and your partnership absolutely "free." Granted, if you are producing a public service announcement, you may need to hire a writer if no one else on your team can write it. If you're going to send photographs to a television station, newspaper or Internet site to support a story or for a TV public service announcement, you might have to hire a photographer. But then again, you probably can get this service donated by a volunteer, employee or local photographer.

To ensure that you get what you want and need for photographs and video from your press conference or other early-on events, provide your own photographer and videographer. Do not hope that you can receive copies of photographs or video taken by the media. Having your own photos and video gives you complete control and allows for the greatest flexibility in your on-going campaign. Prior to any event, provide the photographer/videographer with a specific "shot list" of the people you want to capture, as well as an agenda of the key elements of the event so that they are prepared for what's coming up next. Also make any introductions necessary so that they have easy access to get the photos/video you need.

While there are many reasons Media Relations is at the top of the Marketing Wheel, one that stands out is that the cost of Media Relations can be a fraction of the value that you will receive. In most cases, for every dollar you spend, your return can usually produce upwards of $100. Pretty hard to beat that!

Simply put - Media Relations will place your good works on a public stage and turn the light on. Your organization will not glow unless people know and see what you are doing.

Develop a Comprehensive Media List

As media contacts are always changing, I use an Excel spreadsheet to manage and update my media list. Other database management programs will also work for this purpose. I first categorize my media spreadsheet by type (television, radio, newspaper, magazine, Internet news sites, blog writers, wire services, etc.) Then under the appropriate type heading, I list each media outlet in my marketing territory. This territory could be local for smaller organizations, regional for larger ones, national and international for some. For example, under the television/local heading I would list all television stations within the San Francisco Bay Area, making sure all the ethnic TV stations are included.

And then for each particular media outlet, I have separate listings for the following: news director, assignment editor, community relations director or public affairs director, talk show producer, marketing and/or promotions director, and/or other titles depending on the medium. For each listing, I will have a person's name, direct telephone number, cell phone number if I have it, email address, and physical address. It is also important when pitching a news story or special event to get the direct news line at radio and television stations and their news emails. For example: to email a news story to KGO TV Channel 7 in San Francisco, the ABC affiliate, I use abc7listens@kgo-tv.com, which goes directly to their News Assignment Editor. I email and make a personal phone call to these news lines if, and only if, it is really a news story - something happening now or within the next 24 hours. It is a similar procedure when working with print media (newspapers and internet news primarily) except your primary contact will usually be the City Desk Editor. For example: to send a news story to the San Francisco Examiner, I use the address: newstips@sfexaminer.com.

Find out who produces their public affairs/community talk shows. Start with contacting their public affairs director. Most of these shows are taped during the week and aired on Sunday mornings. And many times interview opportunities are available on certain newscasts or other locally-produced programs during the day. This is where you can place a spokesperson in an interview situation to talk about your cause or project. Every radio and television station is required by Federal broadcast regulations to provide some form of public affairs programming, such as talk shows, public service announcements, a calendar of community events, and other public service and community-benefit messaging. Importantly, all such programming is free for you. Putting together such media lists is a great jello job.

The marketing and/or promotions director is the best contact if you're trying to create a media co-sponsorship, contest, or other on-air promotional opportunity.

The simplest way to find out all this information is to pick up the phone and call the different media. Call their main switchboard and ask for the person's title such as news editor, city editor, community relations director, etc. Then ask this person which telephone number and email is best to reach them when you want to pitch a story, interview or news item. Usually, they are happy to help. An Internet search for the media outlets in your area also will usually provide a detailed list. For example, I did a quick search for "All radio stations in Texas" and came up with *www.ontheradio.net/states/texas*, which listed every Texas radio station and links to its website.

If your project or campaign has a specific date for an event, you will find that almost all media provide some form of an event calendar. These event calendars will need your information anywhere between two and six weeks prior to the event. So check with each individual media outlet for their deadline. A calendar release (sample in **Resource Center**) is a very short who, what, when, where and why announcement. Also look for the independent websites that cover your marketing region. *Craigslist.org* provides a calendar of events section in the regions where they provide their service. Add all of these contacts and names to your master media list.

Also be sure to do a web search for websites and blogs that cover your particular topic area in your greater marketing region. Provide them with a short but topical story or release about your project or cause marketing campaign.

This media list is your Bible in the PR, news and promotion world. It is important that you keep it up-to-date.

Deadlines

When developing your media list, be sure to ask each different contact what their deadline is for their particular area. For example: contacting the media to place a spokesperson on a talk show usually requires a six to eight week lead time; a calendar release three to four weeks; a breaking news story, well obviously, immediately! List these deadlines in your master media list for each particular contact or area.

This is not a complete listing of every Media Relations opportunity, but you get the picture. There are a lot of ways in which you can leverage your strategy and messaging for relatively little cost. In all cases with all media, the less commercial your message the better. If your partnership is promoting that $.10 from every can of soda (or any product or service) goes to a particular nonprofit, the media may not consider this as a public service message, even though it benefits a nonprofit. In many cases they will tell you to buy advertising. And that's a whole other circle! The success of everything listed above depends on how you position your message as a benefit for the cause and for the greater good of the community.

Spokespersons

You'll need to determine who will best serve the important role of spokesperson for your project or cause. In fact, you may have several spokespersons on different topics for different types of public speaking or media interview opportunities. Ideally, this person will be experienced in working with the media, comfortable being on camera and able to deliver concise and meaningful messages about your project or campaign. While you may have several spokespersons including the CEO or Executive Director of your cross-sector partners, it is not necessary to always have the "top dog" as your primary spokesperson, as many times it's hard to get that much time from their schedules. Select among your partners two or three people who have the experience to serve this role well, as this also provides more scheduling options. I've found that it is highly productive to have two or three different spokespeople coming from different perspectives, though talking about the same project or campaign.

For the Health and Wellness Fair in Oakland, we sent reporters and talk show producers one paragraph bios of three different potential spokespersons/interview guests: a CEO who would speak to his company's long history of community involvement; the director of nursing for the Alameda County Public Health Department who could speak to the health and wellness needs of the community; and an executive from the Center for Elders' Independence who could speak about the health and insurance challenges faced by senior citizens. The media had the choice of who was most appropriate for their particular show or story idea. This multiple-spokesperson approach proved to be very successful in garnering significant interview and talk show placements.

Feature Stories

Feature stories can also be developed. For example, if you were promoting, or as it's called in the media world, "pitching," a story for a homeless shelter, it would be best to line up several individuals the reporter could interview, such as the Executive Director, a person being served by the homeless shelter, a local doctor who is providing services to the homeless, and volunteers helping to build the shelter. Feature stories tend to be more about trends and various viewpoints on an important subject, rather than to provide a specific message or call-to-action. So it's best to be prepared with information about the industry, even other people in your same business, when pitching a feature story.

Public Service Announcements (PSAs)

Public Service Announcements (usually called PSAs) are free radio and TV messages usually in one of three versions: 10 seconds, 20 seconds and 30 seconds. In most cases you will write the copy (words) for the PSAs and the station will either record them or have their on-air talent read them during programming. In most cases, public service announcements need to be provided to the media five to six weeks prior to when you wish to have them aired. Because such announcements are free and air-time is limited, there is tremendous competition in getting these placed. You stand a much better chance of placement if your PSAs are well-written, concise, and provide a strong value to the general community. The media will provide guidelines and/or examples for you to follow. I have placed public service announcement examples in the **Resource Center** under Media Relations.

Ethnic Media

According to New American Media, a collaboration of ethnic news organizations, there are approximately 2,000 ethnic media organizations in the United States, connecting approximately 57,000,000 adults. Not only is this a huge population, but this population is very loyal to their particular media, especially when a considerable percentage them don't speak English and must get their news and information in their native language from ethnic media. To overlook ethnic media, and thereby important populations for your marketing campaign, would be a big mistake. For instance, marketing and communications campaigns, nonprofit or for-profit, in the San Francisco Bay Area many times will deliver their messaging in English, Spanish and Chinese (both Cantonese and Mandarin). This focus on the prominent languages spoken in their community is certainly true of most metropolitan areas in the United States.

While many ethnic media, will, out of necessity, accept public service announcements, press releases and other information in English, it is far more productive (and respectful) to provide this information in their own language. Of course, there are translation services you can use, but I've never had to use one. In your pool of partners, stakeholders and volunteers there will undoubtedly be someone who can help with the translating you need. Take advantage of the wealth of marketing and publicity opportunities that are provided by ethnic media.

Media Associations

Many large cities and regions will have associations made up of members of the media, and these associations can be very good friends of your project or campaign. Our area's is the Northern California Broadcasters Association. The primary focus of such media associations is to generate ideas and collaborative advertising campaigns. In other words, their purpose is to generate sales for their association's radio stations and yet they can be very helpful in providing advertising for major cause-related campaigns in their marketing region...so don't overlook this important opportunity to help your campaign.

Public Relations

The key objective of public relations is to create a favorable image and reputation of your organization. It is this favorable image and the enhancement of your brand that will make the public want to learn more about your organization and buy your products or utilize your programs and services. If your PR is stronger and more favorable than your competitor, it is likely that the public will buy from you or support your cause-related campaigns rather than your competitor's.

While public relations and brand promotion of your cause are your focus, the way you attract this awareness is through press relations, speaking at events, serving as a guest on media talk shows, or the luncheon speaker at a Rotary or Kiwanis club, providing educational seminars and trainings, creating linkages with organizations that support your mission, etc. Like media relations, there's a misconception that public relations is free.... it's not. It takes creative strategy and development, staff or volunteer time from your partnership, the cost to develop promotional and public relations materials and a modest cost to underwrite general expenses. But as we discussed in Media Relations, you are not paying for the actual media time you are receiving or mind share you are creating. That part is "free."

Here is where your public relations agency (pro bono or paid) can be of immense service to your partnership.

Special Events

Are special events worth the trouble? That depends. The good news is that a special event can create tremendous excitement, media interest and coverage, public and potential donor interaction with your cause, and even raise funding. The bad news is that special events can take an extraordinary amount of time, staff, volunteers and funding. I remember all too well when I was working with one large nonprofit organization and they were planning their annual fundraising gala. While it was chaired and run by a volunteer committee, the gala required a huge amount of time from marketing, fund development, and other departments of the organization. Many months were spent in planning the event and, in the end, it raised approximately $100,000 after expenses. My conviction then and still today was that this amount of money paled in comparison to what that same staff and volunteer time could have accomplished in fundraising and marketing reach if the effort had been placed on a particular project or two and focused on a greater good… and not a glitzy, ballroom-based, black-tie party that received almost no media or general public coverage, except for one photo on the society page.

Many nonprofits believe that this type of major event is good for donor relations. I feel that there are many better ways to make your donors happy and attract new ones, especially when putting their money to good work and showing them what you've done.

Special events engage the public, attract the media and bring awareness to your program or cause. Just think twice before jumping in with both feet, and analyze the cost/reward ratio of major, glitzy special events.

Press Conferences

Nearly everyone thinks that their event, project or campaign will draw all sorts of attention from the media, and invariably will recommend that a press conference be held. This is a natural reaction due to your excitement about the partnership you've created and the cause endeavor that you are undertaking. However, like any special event, a press conference takes considerable time, planning, staff and cost, and thus should be used only when you really have a major news announcement to make. The media come to press conferences because they're expecting news. If you feel that what you are undertaking can sincerely create news excitement on a local or regional basis, then by all means hold a press conference. You will want to have your top leaders from the partnership there to explain your project or the campaign that you are launching. It is also helpful if you can include your local mayor, city councilmember, fire chief, police chief or other dignitary to help draw attention to the importance of this event and attract the media. However, be forewarned that the attendance of these dignitaries does not necessarily guarantee news coverage. The mayor, for example, may be attending many events every day, so is not necessarily a draw.

Paid Advertising

The best things about paid advertising are that you can craft your message to be delivered exactly how you want, place your ads on the media where you think they will have the greatest impact, schedule the times or locations that they will be shown, and have all guaranteed with a contract between you and the particular media outlet. The downside, of course, is that you have to pay for all of this, and paid advertising can be prohibitively expensive for most cross-sector partnerships.

If you're fortunate enough to have an advertising agency working as part of your team, many doors can be opened to leverage paid advertising. The most obvious point of leverage is the fact that advertising agencies spend their client's money to buy advertising, and major agencies spend millions of dollars on it. However, the media is not always motivated to help you, even if you have an advertising agency on your team because many times they like to keep the sales and editorial sides of their business separate.

The best approach is to have your agency contact their sales rep at the media and ask if there's any way that they might influence coverage for a better deal. Just don't do this yourself. The one big exception to this rule is working with small media outlets, especially weekly newspapers. In many of these cases, sales and editorial are closely linked, so in some cases, if you don't buy an ad you won't get editorial coverage.

Partner Relations and Promotions

The best part of a partnership is that you're not alone. You have the ability to tap the intelligence and resources of all members of your partnership and in many cases, other relationships your partners will bring to support your project or campaign. One of the partners in the Health and Wellness Fair was the Center for Elders' Independence. Because they joined our partnership, we were able to develop an entirely separate section of the Health Fair devoted specifically to seniors and thereby reach out to senior-oriented media for excellent publicity and discounted advertising. Our Health Fair was greatly strengthened and expanded to new audiences because of the educational and promotional opportunities brought to us by this partner.

Explore all opportunities with your partners. They may be able to share their media list or have close working relationships with key members of the media, or have extensive databases to deliver the messages of your campaign. They will have communications vehicles such as newsletters, annual reports, quarterly updates, direct mail, blogs, social media, e-mail communications, etc. Combining all of these potential audiences, you're talking about a significant amount of people who could receive and be motivated by your campaign messaging.

Guerilla Marketing

I have put guerilla marketing in its own category, even though it usually involves some form of event and certainly engages the use of media relations, public relations and other aspects of the Marketing Wheel. Guerilla marketing is a tactic focused on generating immediate public interest, usually through an unexpected, in-your-face event. For example: A group of supposedly random people in a shopping mall all of a sudden undertaking a coordinated song and dance routine, referred to as a "flash mob," is a form of guerilla marketing. Marketers use these unexpected events to generate viral awareness and news coverage to promote their products and services. Guerilla marketing is at its best when it's unconventional, thought-provoking, imaginative and buzz-generating, while delivering the marketing message you want to convey.

Websites

Each of your participating partners will have websites that the partnership should utilize to help spread the message of your project or campaign. I recommend that you develop a webpage devoted specifically to your partnership, project or campaign. For example, this page could be listed as *www.shelterforthehomeless.org/newshelter* or on your partner's site, something like: *www.Ramosbuilding.com/new shelter*. On this page you will want to provide:

- A concise description of your project or campaign, with goals, timetables, etc.

- A description of each of the partnering organizations and a link to their website

- If possible, photos or renderings of what you are building or doing

- A prominent button or link in a bright color (red is perfect) to a donation page (such as PayPal or other online donation collector)

- A place for volunteers to register, if you need volunteers from outside the partnership

- A link to news stories that have been placed concerning the project

- Short biographies of people serving as your campaign's spokespersons

- Contact information, including phone number, e-mail, and possibly a person's name for additional information

Each partner's website should link the reader directly to the project or campaign's home page. Your campaign website should be updated whenever "news" happens (you've broken ground for the building), you've reached a particular milestone (your funding goals were met), and the like. Always post photographs alongside each stage to provide the visitor with a visual timeline presentation of your progress. Once you have all your partners sharing this information with people visiting their websites, the cross-pollination of these website links will raise your search engine optimization (SEO). That's the fancy way of saying Google, Bing, and Yahoo, among others will list you higher and people will find you faster.

There are many free website platforms that you can use for your campaign's site. These platforms provide templates for design, adding photography and text, and all else that you will need to develop a highly attractive and effective website. My recommendation is to use WordPress. I use it for my personal blog (*www.burtch.wordpress.com*) and a huge number of organizations and individuals use WordPress as their website platform. One of the best reasons for using WordPress, besides its being free and easy to design and navigate, is that the major search engines love WordPress.

Printed Material

To help spread the messaging and images of your project or campaign, having printed material to pass out is very helpful. Being able to control exactly how you want to communicate your messages and designing those messages to your particular audiences, including presenting your materials in different languages, gives you total power over how you want the public and your other stakeholders to see your project or campaign presented. As much as we try, publicity approaches often cannot communicate your message as comprehensively or as accurately as you would like. Flyers, posters, banners, e-mail newsletters, direct mail and other forms of printed or electronically-distributed materials will deliver your message in multiple formats and exactly how you designed them. While four-color, glossy printed brochures make for an excellent presentation, they can be expensive and sometimes deliver the wrong message. When you're undertaking a campaign that requires raising funds, you do not want to communicate that you are spending a lot of money on fancy collateral material. With digital technology and relatively low-cost, high-speed color printers, you can produce exceptional collateral material at very reasonable prices.

Social Media

Social media covers a lot of ground: Twitter, Facebook, YouTube, mobile applications/texting, blogs, podcasts, Foursquare, Google+, Instagram, Pinterest, crowdsourcing...and a whole lot more. There has been so much written about social media and so many good sources of information that can be found through an Internet search (and in the **Resource Center** under Social Media) that I will not go into a long explanation here. Needless to say, social media opportunities are exploding and can work exceptionally well when communicating and engaging people in a good cause. Creating an online community to support your organization and in particular, your partnership's cause-related project or campaign, should be part of your Marketing Plan.

As we discussed earlier in the section on cause marketing, the American Red Cross took full advantage of social media through an innovative texting program following the earthquake devastation in Haiti and Hurricane Sandy, as did the more local *I Am Here* campaign in Austin, Texas.

My one word of caution is that the use of social media needs to be put into its proper perspective, by which I mean that spending an inordinate amount of time and effort on developing an online community can sometimes overshadow or possibly neglect other very important aspects of your Marketing Plan. For example: if your project or campaign is focused on one local or regional area, the focus of each area/discipline of your Marketing Plan will be directed toward having the largest and most productive impact to the target populations of that local or regional area. I don't suggest you give too much effort focusing on people in other parts of the state, country or world who you might be able to reach via social media but who would have little to no effect on the success of a particular local/regional campaign.

If your partnership is able to develop a comprehensive email list of potential donors, supporters, supplies, media contacts, stakeholders, etc., using e-mail is a far more direct and effective form of communication to these critical audiences than Twitter, Facebook, or other such social media platforms. Of course, the very best approach is to integrate social media with your other marketing efforts.

I've seen many campaigns place so much emphasis on developing a social media platform and community that they have overlooked and sometimes totally disregarded other areas of the Marketing Wheel that would have had a stronger impact on their partnership's success. Building and maintaining a social network/community is a time-consuming, people-requiring process, so be careful here when resources (time, staff and money) are limited.

Working with Celebrities

There is an understandable desire to involve celebrities in your project or campaign. However, this can be a double-edged sword. The good news is that celebrities can draw attention to your cause, your project or campaign. Their photograph on your printed material will create instant recognition. If they agree to do public service announcements, appear in advertising for you, or make a personal appearance at your press conference or groundbreaking, these can all add to the glamour and potential news and public interest in your project.

One of the negatives in using celebrities, however, is that they have been used in a lot of cause-related campaigns and in many cases, the public has become skeptical of celebrity endorsements. Indeed, many people believe that celebrities give these endorsements only because they were paid. This belief can kill all credibility of their endorsement. You can avoid this potentially negative impression if the celebrity has an honest story that relates to your cause. For example, s/he has suffered or has a relative who has suffered from the medical issue/ cause that you are addressing (e.g. Michael J. Fox's focus on finding a cure for Parkinson's disease), or possibly there is video coverage of them helping build a home, playing soccer with Special Olympics athletes or some other proof that the individual truly believes in this particular cause. If this is the case, celebrity endorsements can be especially powerful.

It's important to mention that not all celebrities are the typical Hollywood, music or sports celebrities. There are many well-known individuals that you might want to recruit for your cause, such as politicians, scientists, authors and others. The key is finding the best alignment between the person and your cause, making sure that it's appropriate. For one public service campaign, we included a 10-year-old boy who was the youngest person ever to swim from Alcatraz Island, home of San Francisco's infamous prison, to the San Francisco shoreline. We felt this boy would be an excellent spokesperson for both youth and their parents...and he was tremendous. Sometimes it's much better to have real people who have a real reason to participate in and promote your organization's campaign.

While celebrities may donate their appearance fee, in many cases you'll have to pay their union fees for whichever film, music, actors or other association they belong to. Or in cases of having an entertainer for an event, they may provide their services free but you will usually have to pay for their musicians, travel, food, "beverages", union fees, the roadies and other crewmembers that are a part of their operation and other expenses. If the celebrity donation/attendance draw is large enough, these additional costs may be reasonable compared to the impact their involvement would create for your cause.

Integrating Your Marketing Elements

I want to emphasize the importance of integration. There will be considerable overlap in the marketing elements as you develop the different areas, and this is good. Each and every one of the elements and marketing disciplines of your Marketing Wheel should be integrated with each other to the fullest extent possible. For example, press releases, slogans, key talking points, PowerPoint presentations and collateral material you develop for your press conference can be also be used throughout the execution of your project or campaign. The same goes as you develop photography and video. The photographs and video your photographer/videographer take at the press conference, especially interviews with your key spokesperson and the people you will be serving by your new project, can also be used on your websites, in your press releases, your advertisements, public service announcements, social media, newsletters, e-mail blasts and all forms of your written, visual, online or electronic communication. By pre-planning and then integrating the development of these elements and materials, you will save time and money because you can develop most of them at the same time, at one cost, and use them over and over again.

Finalizing Your Marketing Plan

You are now ready to create a written-out, integrated Marketing Plan, incorporating your creative and tactical strategies, the results of your problem solving and creative development process, and your exploration of the many opportunities within the Marketing Wheel. Remember: You are not writing the Magna Carta. Your Marketing Plan should be concise, easy to understand and easy to communicate to others. There is no need to put anything in this plan that is not absolutely necessary to the execution of its parts. Like a blueprint, you want clear direction that your team can build upon...and nothing else.

This Marketing Plan should include:

- A concise description of the project or campaign that the partnership will undertake, and why this project or campaign is important to the cause and to the benefit of your community

- Your primary objective, and if necessary, your second and third objectives, so there is no misunderstanding of the specific goals and mission of your partnership

- A concise but complete explanation of your creative and tactical strategies

- A description of each element of each area of the Marketing Wheel you wish to undertake

- The specific order and operational timetable in which you will roll out these strategies and elements over the course of your campaign, including monthly goals to be met, whether it's a three-month or two-year campaign

- Who has specific responsibility for the development and management of each particular element or area of the Marketing Plan

- The budget the partnership has allotted to cover the costs of each element and the total budget for the campaign itself

- Who will provide the financing and the approval payment process for projected expenses

- Who will have overall responsibility for managing the entire Marketing Plan/campaign This could be one person or a small subcommittee of the overall partnership team, but I recommend no more than three people maximum

Tap Your Entire Marketing Team

You just never know where the best ideas are going to come from. They could be from your marketing department, PR team, or members of your core partnership team. But when you think about all of your employees, Board of Directors, volunteers, business partners and more, you realize that you have an amazing collection of minds to tap...so tap them! Before you finalize your Marketing Plan, I suggest that you write up your creative and operational strategies in a concise overview, and add to that the areas of the Marketing Wheel that you have decided to pursue. E-mail this document as a "Draft Marketing Plan" to many of your senior management, key employees, volunteers and board. Ask these people to review the plan, add their thoughts, and especially any out-of-the-box thinking. Ask them to provide personal contacts related to any aspect or element of the Marketing Plan. By sending an email, they will have an electronic form of the document, which will make it easier for them to add their ideas and send them back to you. Be sure to caution them not to share this Draft Marketing Plan with anyone outside of their or your organization.

A few things will likely happen:

- You most probably will receive some excellent, maybe even outlandish (and that's a good thing) ideas pertaining to the different areas of your Marketing Wheel. You might want to hold a contest for the best ideas. I have seen this work very well when a dinner and a movie were offered as a grand prize, and gift certificates to coffeehouses or other relatively inexpensive prizes were offered for other good ideas.

- Your stakeholders may have connections to people within the media, pro bono agencies, graphic design firms/printers, or many other valuable contacts that could be invited to join your team and support your project or campaign.

- The very best reason to tap your entire stakeholder team is simply to engage them. By reaching out to them, you are clearly communicating their importance to your organization, to this cross-sector partnership and to this particular project or campaign. They want to feel included and valued, and they will respond accordingly.

When I was with Marriott Corporation in charge of the opening promotion of the Marriott's Great America Park, I was asked by a TV reporter: "How many people do you have on your PR staff?" I said, "3,000." And I meant it. The construction workers building the park, the employees who were being hired, the many vendors who were supplying products and services – this was our PR team and they were excited about being part of such an exciting project. And they spread the good news about Marriott's Great America to tens of thousands of others in the marketing region of our new theme park, which greatly increased our chances for success.

Once your Marketing Plan is complete and approved, send it to the entire partnership team and key stakeholders. Your final Marketing Plan will also provide assurances to your leadership, that of your partner's and to other stakeholders that this campaign was well-conceived and that all costs to possibly impact their organization should provide a high return on their investment. In other words, you want and need their buy-in to this final Marketing Plan.

Stuff Happens

One last note on your Marketing Plan: No surprise, but things change, new ideas will come up, new partners may want to join in, etc. For example, the Center for Elders' Independence was not part of the initial partnership team when we were developing the Health and Wellness Fair in Oakland. However, when we learned of their interest and that by including them in the partnership we would expand our reach to a significant audience of seniors, we jumped all over this new opportunity.

The same goes when you find something is not working or becomes just too difficult to put together. In a partnership I was developing between the USS Potomac Association and the Red and White Fleet of San Francisco, though a seemingly an extraordinarily mutually-beneficial opportunity, in reality we were faced with Port of San Francisco fees, limitations on dockage of such a large ship, and other challenges which greatly limited the potential of the partnership.

Bottom-line: Don't be afraid of new ideas, as long as they are directly related to your strategy. Be prepared to amaze yourselves!

Evaluation and ROI

Evaluation

Looking back on projects, programs or campaigns you have done before, perhaps you can see where changes could have been made along the way if you stopped and sometimes had the courage to raise your hand and say, "Let's look at this situation another way." What differences would that evaluation-in-progress have made in your results?

One of the best four-letter words in cross-sector partnerships is: STOP! At times we get so intense in our work that we don't stop to evaluate where we have been, where we are, and where we need to go next. This necessity for evaluation is critical on several levels. First and foremost, to assure the partnership that you are on track toward the goals you've set up in your strategy and Marketing Plan. Are you on course for success? At regular intervals throughout your project or campaign's progress, you must stop, bring the partnership team together and evaluate what's working and what's not.

To be most effective in evaluating your progress, you need to have a valid baseline upon which to start. I recommend that as part of your final Marketing Plan, you include specific metrics and measurement processes that you will follow throughout the development of your project or campaign. Before we began an emergency preparedness marketing campaign for the Red Cross (a case study follows shortly) we conducted a survey finding that only six percent of San Francisco Bay Area residents were "Red Cross prepared" for a major disaster. And at the beginning and conclusion of each of the three years of the campaign, we surveyed our target audiences to understand where we stood against our goals. Without these surveys and knowing where we were, we would not have been able to tweak the campaign or realize that we were on the right path to significant success.

You will need to decide on which areas are most important for you to measure. The following list will provide sample guidelines as to what you might measure throughout your project and campaign's development. At the end of your effort you should provide a final tabulation of each measurement area for the partnership's review.

- Total dollar amount raised in donations
- Total increase in product or service sales
- Increased brand awareness
- Number of people that were trained or came into your organization seeking assistance or just doing what your campaign asked them to do
- Number of public service announcements and media impressions that you received during your campaign
- Value of the free media coverage you received (Note: There are formulas that give you a fair value both for articles in PR value or what that space would have cost if it was a paid advertisement. Conduct an Internet search for: "What is the advertising value of publicity?" and you will find several links to these formulas.)
- New markets that were opened up because of this project or campaign
- Increased engagement of new audiences, such as Millennials or seniors
- Number of volunteers that were attracted to your project

- Number of employee volunteer hours provided by each partner

- Number of external volunteer hours provided

- Raised level of employee satisfaction due to participation in project or campaign

- Number of coupons that were redeemed or pinups sold

- Number of fans or likes on your Facebook page

- Number of new members who joined your organization

- Increased engagement and investment in your organization by new investors or major donors

- Lowered marketing costs due to effectiveness of campaign

- Increase or decrease in the level of commitment by all partners

Depending on the type of project or campaign you're developing, there will be other areas to evaluate and provide measurement. Remember, all along the way you must test your assumptions against your measurement factors. How else can you measure success?

ROI (Return on Investment)

Trying to obtain quantitative return on investment (ROI) results for social programs, cross-sector partnerships and cause marketing is challenging at best. There is no exact science. Yet in many cases the leadership of the partnering organizations will want to have an ROI report following the completion of a project or campaign or first phase of multiyear partnership to help justify the effort involved. For our purposes, I want to offer two basic ways to approach return on investment for cause marketing and cross-sector partnerships:

- The less intensive approach would be to measure and analyze the many areas I have suggested above as they relate to your project or campaign. This approach is more focused on whether you received value based on your objectives. For example, if your project was completed on time and on budget, if your campaign greatly increased the number of volunteer hours provided to the project or nonprofit partner, or if donations raised for the project were above your costs, these would be an easily measured value resulting from the partnership and a good measure of your success and ROI.

- The more in-depth approach of measuring ROI is to take all factors possible into the accounting equation and see whether or not the partnership created specific financial benefit or business value to your organization and to the partner's organizations. In other words, by "business value" - did the partnership, after all costs are factored in, increase financial revenue for the partner organizations or decrease their business expenses so there was a net positive gain?

One of the country's leading experts in this area of ROI evaluation and measurement is Farron Levy, President and Founder of True Impact. True Impact provides web-based tools and consulting support to help organizations measure the social, financial, and environmental return on investment of their programs and operations. As one of this book's guest experts, Farron has provided excellent information on the second, more thorough approach - measuring Corporate Social Responsibility (CSR), cross-sector partnerships and/or cause marketing programs in terms of financial benefit and business value. His paper, *A Practical Framework for Measuring Social and Business Value* and a *Bottom Line Outcome Measures*, which provides an equation of revenues, cost and social value, can be found in the **Resource Center** under Measuring Return on Investment.

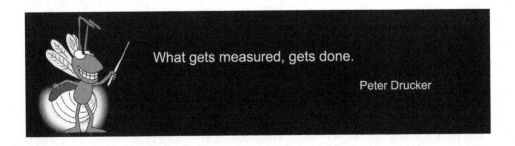

What gets measured, gets done.

Peter Drucker

ROI for Employee Volunteer Programs

I want to complete this section on return on investment with a focus on employee volunteer programs. As I have emphasized throughout this book, the opportunity to raise employee morale and thus increase their retention is one of the major opportunities in the development of cross-sector partnerships. There has been increasing emphasis and research on this important area of employee involvement in cause-related, nonprofit community activities. Senior management and Human Resource departments of organizations providing such employee volunteer opportunities are looking for ways to measure the return on investment against the cost of such activities. This has given rise to a relatively new area of "employee volunteer standards." The Points of Light Institute, in partnership with several nonprofit, for-profit, and foundation participants, produced the *2010 Employee Volunteer Program Reporting Standards*. This document provides a wealth of information and guidelines on measuring the return on investment for employee volunteer programs. For example, the report discusses both the straight return on investment (ROI) and also what is called the social return on investment (SROI) of employee volunteer programs.

The full Points of Light Institute report can be found in the **Resource Center** under Employee Volunteer Programs. Measuring social media ROI can also prove to be challenging, so I also recommend that you read "20 Free Social Media Monitoring Tools you should be Using," which is located at *smallbiztrends.com/2012/09/20-free-social-media-monitoring-tools.html*

Years ago when I was volunteering with San Francisco Special Olympics, we wanted to increase the number of athletes participating in our programs. My public relations agency (The William Bentley Agency) provided pro bono services, working with KGO TV, the San Francisco ABC affiliate, and the Special Olympics Board of Directors. Together we developed a registration drive campaign called "Join the Winners' Circle," with the goal of attracting as many new athletes to the program as possible. We set up as our measurable goals:

Goals to be measured	Results
• Increase registration of new Special Olympics athletes	46% increase in registration
• Increase new volunteers	30% increase in volunteers

In addition, this campaign generated exceptional public interest in Special Olympics through the public service announcements on KGO television and other media outlets, and this campaign served as an outstanding introduction for a new major gifts fund development program which was launched following the registration drive. The campaign was so successful that a detailed "how-to" guidebook was developed and sent to every major Special Olympics chapter in the United States, underwritten by the Kennedy Foundation.

Funding Plan

Adequate financial support is required to meet the goals of your partnership. Generally speaking, this support comes from partner funding and external funding. Your partner funding is the internal financial support to develop and run your cross-sector partnership, project or cause marketing campaign. Your external funding is the financial support that your campaign will be designed to attract from the general public, foundations, corporations, and other funding entities. While this book is not intended to provide a course in fundraising, I will provide some guidelines and direction on how to approach this critically important element.

Partner Funding

Prior to the completion and certainly prior to the execution of your Marketing Plan, you will need to raise the funding for the campaign budget to cover the initial and potentially all the elements of your plan. In most cases, this funding will come from the corporate partner(s). For the American Red Cross partnership with Pacific Gas & Electric campaign (case study in next section), the vast majority of funding came from a three-year grant from Pacific Gas & Electric. However, the Red Cross provided staff time of their marketing department, training teams, accounting and other personnel and overhead costs, which became part of the overall budget expenditures. These costs in personnel, supplies, overhead and other expenses must be accounted for in your financial planning.

Your financing requirements are not always the sole responsibility of your for-profit partners. In several campaigns cash funding and in-kind donations have come from nonprofit organizations who contributed due to the benefit that their organization and their mission would receive. Yes, your nonprofit, education or possibly government partners will probably invest far more in staff time and other non-cash resources, but at least explore if these organizations might also provide some financial assistance to the overall campaign or project.

You do not want to develop a Marketing Plan that reaches beyond your ability to pay for it. And you certainly don't want to get halfway through your campaign or project and run out of money. That's like building half a bridge.

So don't go into any project, campaign or program without having all of your expenses planned and covered first. It's far better to scale back ambitious plans to a point where you are fully confident that you are able to execute your plan. Successfully completing the first project or Phase 1 of a multi-year campaign and being able to show this success to the public, all of your stakeholders, and especially your funders, will set the stage for the successful funding and completion of a potential next project or Phase 2.

Don't take on too much too fast - no bridge is better than building half a bridge.

External Funding

In almost all cases, your campaign will include an external fundraising effort. In the section on the different types of cause marketing campaigns, we discussed ways to raise money, such as a pinup campaign, online donations and several others. In your assessment leading up to the development of your strategy and marketing campaign, you should have decided what type of external (non-partner) fundraising approach you will use.

Although I advise against spending too much time applying for foundation or corporate grants, if someone on your board or another supporter holds an influential position within a corporate or independent foundation, or knows somebody well who does, by all means explore this potential. You should plan on a six-12 month funding cycle for this granting process, unless your advocate can personally influence and possibly shorten this typical timetable.

In the majority of projects or campaigns, you will want to encourage donations from the public. Through your public service announcements, paid advertising (if available), printed collateral material, certainly on your website (see next section) and whenever a spokesperson is on a talk show, media interview or speaking engagement, the need for public donations to your project or campaign should be highlighted in this messaging. Most importantly, say how the audience can donate.

If your cause is of significant size, such as raising funds for an international natural disaster, an epidemic, HIV/AIDS or other program that affects a large population, holding special events in restaurants, performance centers, and other public venues can prove to be an excellent approach for raising funds. The same approach can also be used with much smaller, more local campaigns. For example, if you want to support a child with cancer, a local school or a family who lost their home and all their belongings in a fire, you could hold house parties, small dinner gatherings, events at local restaurants, etc. This is where your friends, partners, employees, and local supporters can be of great help participating in or coordinating a hands-on fundraising event.

The Challenge of Foundations

Most professional fundraisers and nonprofit development directors (of which I am neither) cringe when I say that I personally feel that a large amount of effort is often wasted by nonprofit organizations seeking foundation grants. Having worked with several of the largest corporate and independent foundations in the country, I know that they are inundated with requests for funding from the nonprofit community, and the line is getting longer. There also is a growing trend for foundations (corporate and independent) to focus on specific areas on which to concentrate their funding. In many cases, foundations are not seeking to develop a long-term partnership with another organization. Now there are exceptions, but the majority of corporate and independent foundations may fund a project or initiative, but do not provide volunteers, coordinate in-kind donations, lend highly skilled executives, or the myriad of other benefits we have explored previously as part of the relationship between your organization and a cross-sector partner.

If your cross-sector partnership program or campaign falls within the specific funding guidelines of a local or national foundation, and you have a well-connected friend or someone on the inside of a foundation to help guide you, then investigate the potential of this funding. I just recommend that you don't spend too much time standing in that long line.

Online Fundraising

It is imperative that you make it easy for people to donate to your project or campaign. Put a donation button/link prominently on your websites to direct readers to a page that clearly explains the project, the partners, and especially, the cause. There are several platforms that you can incorporate within your website to collect funding such as Causes, which is integrated into Facebook, Donate Now/Network for Good, Fundly, Rally, DonorsChoose, and many more. It is also very easy to put a PayPal button/link on your site. This is where social media can be of great support. Utilize your Facebook, Twitter and other social media platforms to communicate your message and drive people to your donation page. And all other aspects of your Marketing Plan should direct people to the same place.

In all cases, donations provided to your project or campaign should be immediately acknowledged with a thank you note (please, not an e-mail - a real paper note/letter). Senna, the daughter of a good friend of mine, wanted to raise money to save the baby sea lions that were being stranded and dying off the California coast. So she set up a campaign through the online platform GoFundMe.com in the hopes of raising $350, which seemed like a very ambitious goal to a seven-year-old girl. Her campaign website featured a very cute picture she drew of a seal lion pup. (Note strong emotional pull!) I sent in a donation through the website and approximately one week later I received a personal thank you letter in the mail from Senna, with a copy of her picture and a note that the campaign had reached nearly $800 and was still growing. It doesn't get any better than that.

Whatever you do, do not include a pitch for more money in a thank you note! This happens all the time, which I think is horrible. With their contact information and financial support of your project or cause, you have begun a relationship, one that should be nurtured throughout the life of the project or campaign and beyond.

As you explore different funding approaches, be sure to examine how your nonprofit or education partners are currently raising funding for their organizations. For example: What is the size of their current donor base; what is the range of donations from large to small; what are the total annual contributions; how do they communicate with their donors, through e-mail, regular mail, newsletters, etc. You are looking for the funding approaches and forms of communication that they have in existence now. This will help you determine how to utilize this information as part of your campaign.

Obviously, this is just an overview of ways to have your project or campaign funded from both internal and external sources. Fund development is a profession in and of itself, but it's not that complicated when you have a good cause, use the right messaging and donation platforms and have good people to help.

bCause™ by Socxs™

Over the years I have been approached by many people introducing new technologies or new approaches for marketing, fund development and social media. They have wanted my review as to the relevance of their new product or service to my marketplace - primarily for-profit and nonprofit organizations. First and foremost, I am not that technical, but I do understand a good idea when I see one. I was introduced to the CEO and founder of Socxs, and not to be too cute, but this technology knocked my socks off! The team behind Socxs is top-tier technologists and they have integrated all forms of social media, web and mobile communications into a brand-promoting technology platform for a person or organization. They also came up with a brand name I wish I had thought of: bCause™.

bCause™ provides a unifying platform to integrate the power of web, social and mobile technologies, allowing nonprofit brands to create new markets, increase donor engagement and drive more personal, year-round funding opportunities. bCause creates a unique interactive relationship between the nonprofit, the volunteer and the contributor. Powered by Socxs™, bCause™ stimulates grassroots fundraising by simplifying donor acquisition, tracking, and two-way communication.

Being able to instantly empower personal volunteer networks with social media is a compelling new paradigm for fundraising. With bCause, every volunteer builds his/her own individual network through personal outreach among friends, family and co-workers while collectively supporting their chosen nonprofit organization. bCause™ turns each volunteer into a personal champion for the cause while also acknowledging the volunteer for their personal efforts on behalf of the cause.

I was so impressed that I have moved all my social media, web presence, mobile, etc. to bCause, because I feel it will hyper-accelerate my brand recognition and create an interactive, push/pull messaging opportunity for my partnership-building business. Socxs works just as well with for-profit organizations. Check them out at *www.socxs.com*.

Implementation

Game on! At this point you will have all the partners on board, stakeholders engaged, project or campaign decisions made, Marketing Plan finalized, funding secured or in the pipeline. You have the many supportive resources in the Resource Center, such as the forms, sample communication templates, content from our guest experts, and much more. You have everything you need to begin developing your own highly successful cross-sector partnerships, and most importantly, you are on your way to having your organization glow.

So in the Immortal Words of Nike - *Just Do It!*

You are now in full implementation mode. Whatever challenges come up, your relationships are strong and you can handle them. When new ideas or opportunities arise, you are prepared to run them by your strategy, your budget and timetable to see if they should be added, disregarded or held off for the next project or campaign. As the momentum begins to build, as your plans begin to take shape, you will find an energy and excitement that is rare in the business (any business) world because you know that all this effort will produce results for all partners and for the greater good you are serving.

Most importantly during the implementation phase, keep your communications flowing and your budgets and timelines on track while remaining flexible and keeping relationships trusting and caring. These necessary elements of success will serve you well in the process of meeting and exceeding your key objectives.

I have been involved in developing partnerships of all sizes and variations, and each and every one of these was unique, exciting and sometimes a bit nerve-racking. Each pushed the partnership team to the limit of their engagement and creativity, and because of that, created results beyond our wildest imaginations in nearly every case. Of course, there were a few exceptions, though in 35 years of building partnerships, only a very few.

Case Study: *Prepare Bay Area*

As we've seen throughout this book, when the right partners come together focused on the greater good, magic can happen. The following case study explains in detail the implementation of a campaign that brought together two very different primary partners who, focused on a singular mission, hit on all creative and tactical cylinders and accomplished an unprecedented achievement.

The partnership was between the American Red Cross Bay Area chapter and Pacific Gas & Electric Company (PG&E). As you go through this case study, you will see that we employed an unusually large amount of marketing opportunities and tactics to motivate our audiences. But most importantly, every aspect of this campaign was based upon a very tight creative strategy, tactical roll-out and timeline. If you're a small or midsized organization, look at how the success of this campaign was based almost entirely on its creativity, its motivating messages and finding the right partners. Organizations of any size can proportionately achieve such success.

Background of the Issue

In 2004, the US Geological Survey predicted that a catastrophic earthquake would hit the San Francisco Bay Area within the next 30 years. Which could also mean...in the next 30 seconds! In 2005, following this report, the American Red Cross Bay Area chapter commissioned an independent survey finding that only six percent of Bay Area residents were prepared for a major emergency. Six percent! The San Francisco Bay Area experiences small earthquakes all the time and with the significant media coverage through the years since the devastating 1906 earthquake it was clear that most everyone was aware of the impending threat. The problem was that Bay Area residents had become complacent and weren't doing anything about preparing for the next "Big One." And yet the "Big One" is going to be catastrophic. Estimates are that 3,400 people will die, 63,000 injured and 400,000-500,000 will be made homeless....all within 15 seconds of a catastrophic earthquake. Something had to be done!

Partners

I was Director of Marketing & Communications for the American Red Cross Bay Area at the time. With a dismal six percent of the Bay Area being prepared, we decided to develop a combined public awareness and training program that would address this potential, possibly impending catastrophe. As the Red Cross is a first responder in such disaster situations, our goal was to significantly increase the number of Bay Area households prepared for a major earthquake or any other form of significant disaster. Because it was truly a life or death situation, we were highly motivated.

There was just one problem, or more like two: our Red Cross chapter did not have the training staff capacity to undertake such an enormous training program. And the Red Cross could not provide the funding necessary to undertake a comprehensive Bay Area-wide promotional and cause marketing campaign. We needed a corporate partner who had both the financial resources and a vested interest in preparing the San Francisco Bay Area public for a disaster.

We didn't have far too look. Whenever a major disaster hits, the local utility company is hit very hard, with downed power lines, broken gas mains, people not knowing whether or not to turn off their household gas lines, etc. So we approached our regional utility, Pacific Gas & Electric Company, because they had the aligned mission to inform and prepare people in case of a major emergency, let alone a catastrophic earthquake. Meeting together, we realized that we had the opportunity to undertake such a massive effort, if we combined our knowledge and abilities. We formed a very strong partnership and together developed a program called *Prepare Bay Area.*

We then set the audacious, certainly unprecedented goal of training one million Bay Area residents in emergency preparedness. In Red Cross terms, *being prepared* meant that residents:

- Made an emergency plan, which included exit plans from their residence, and developing a communications link with friends and relatives outside of the Bay Area, and more

- Built an emergency supply kit of food, water, radio, flashlights and other emergency supplies

- Were trained in CPR and other life-saving information

PG&E provided a one million dollar grant over three years to support the Prepare Bay Area initiative. Together the Red Cross and PG&E developed a two-pronged tactical approach to our goal of training 1,000,000 people, which by the way, meant that we would have to train approximately 25% of the people living in the four-county region covered by the American Red Cross Bay Area chapter. It's hard to put such an unprecedented goal in perspective.

Our first tactical approach was to greatly increase the internal Red Cross capability to manage the training of such a very large number of Bay Area residents in emergency preparedness. With approximately 90% of the PG&E funding being allocated to the training program, we were able to hire two full-time employees specifically tasked to coordinate the existing training staff of the Red Cross, develop the training materials and help manage the significant support staff of volunteers who were our feet-on-the-street for the public trainings.

Our second tactical approach was to develop a Bay Area-wide media/promotional campaign to motivate the general public, corporate, educational, nonprofit and governmental organizations to take the life-saving training provided by the Red Cross. It was my job to create and manage the media/promotional campaign and motivate the obviously complacent public to do something they've never done before… prepare for a major earthquake or any kind of a disaster by completing our three-step process.

Why Did Pacific Gas & Electric Join This Partnership?

It is very important for this case study exploration, and for your development of cross-sector partnerships to understand why PG&E would join this partnership and commit one million dollars over three years to support the *Prepare Bay Area* campaign. Ezra Garrett, Vice President, Community Relations and Executive Director, PG&E Corporation Foundation, shares their thinking, "A priority for PG&E's community investment program is to identify initiatives where we can provide our experience and expertise – above and beyond our financial support – to help address critical community needs. So as a utility company and first responder when disasters strike, the American Red Cross and the *Prepare Bay Area* Campaign were a natural fit." He added, "In addition, the Red Cross applied real rigor in their assessment of the preparedness needs of the Bay Area community and articulated a strategy that we felt could deliver significant positive impact at scale. These were the fundamental drivers that enabled our one million dollar commitment to support the effort."

As we have discussed throughout this book, each partner comes into a cross-sector partnership with specific objectives which they would like to achieve. So what did PG&E hope to accomplish through this campaign? Ezra explained: "Our customers have very high expectations of PG&E as it relates to our support for the community. They want to see us actively engaged in efforts to strengthen the neighborhoods that we serve, and the Prepare Bay Area's high profile campaign really helped to shine a light on PG&E's community involvement work. PG&E was co-branded with the American Red Cross throughout the duration of the three-year campaign, and as the campaign touched more and more people, we saw a commensurate improvement in the level of customer awareness of PG&E's work in the community. This improvement supported an increase in overall customer favorability for the company over that period." Yes, PG&E, which has had a mixed reputation with the public, got involved in part to improve its favorability ratings.

We knew we needed creative help on such a significant campaign, and we found a great partner in Publicis & Hal Riney, one of the nation's leading advertising agencies, based in San Francisco. Approaching a major advertising or public relations agency with such a huge pro bono request was shooting for the top, and we knew it. Despite our enthusiasm to develop an unusual campaign, the seriousness of the need facing our greater community and the fact that their CEO, Karen Francis, was a supporter of the Red Cross, this was not going to be an easy sell.

I was introduced to Karen by our CEO, Harold Brooks, and when we sat down she said something that is one of the key lessons in the whole area of pro bono relationships. She told me how busy her creative team was and that the work for Red Cross would be taking serious time away from large, money-making advertising projects that they already had. Then she told me they would give us one idea for a campaign, and only one. If we liked the idea, we would work together and develop it to the fullest extent possible. If we didn't like the idea, we would part as friends...but that was all they were going to offer. A fair offer, to be sure.

However, it didn't turn out quite that way. When their creative team started brainstorming, the ideas started to flow, then explode! Their Creative Director became fixated on this project, to the point of Karen telling me that it was taking a lot of time away from their regular projects. But their excitement was so high, and the ideas were so astonishing that she kept the green light on. At the final creative presentation, with Karen Francis sitting there, the creative team unveiled not one, not two, but three entirely different creative campaign concepts, with multiple elements within each. It was overwhelming, just simply amazing. For the next couple of hours we cut and pasted from those three campaign concepts and bundled together the most creative and certainly one of the most effective cause marketing campaigns I have ever seen, which you are about to see.

Creative Strategy Development

We knew that to get the public engaged and motivated to prepare for an earthquake, we needed to really shake things up...pun intended.

We also knew that given our limited marketing budget (approximately $100,000 over three years) against such a huge task, that our campaign strategy would have to be extremely creative. It would have to excite the Bay Area media so they would communicate our messages to the public for free. After exploring out-of-the-box concepts from Publicis & Hal Riney and adding some great ideas from our very creative Red Cross marketing team, we decided upon our campaign's creative strategy. We named it: "What do we have to do to get your attention?" Now this slogan was for our internal creative direction, not for our external media and promotional messaging. This creative strategy drove all aspects for our campaign. It also set the tone and style of our tactical approaches for the campaign, as the idea was to present a somewhat extreme, shock and awe, in-your-face guerilla marketing approach that would grab the public's attention, and hopefully, motivate the public to take the free Red Cross training. We felt that nothing short of this high intensity, frontal attack would motivate a Bay Area population so used to earthquake threats and warnings.

The *Prepare Bay Area* media and promotional campaign was multi-disciplined, multi-event and tightly integrated. The following will provide a brief overview of the primary marketing and creative elements and the tactical approach we executed for this campaign.

Please visit the *Prepare Bay Area* section of the **Resource Center** to see four-color renderings of all of the samples and to watch an absolutely must-see video of the billboard and people's reactions produced by Jason Boyce, a Red Cross volunteer.

Press Announcement and Conference

We began the campaign by sending out a mock newspaper to all Bay Area media outlets, announcing that an 8.1 earthquake had hit the San Francisco Bay Area and that the Red Cross was calling a press conference for the following morning in downtown San Francisco. Note: The 1906 earthquake which devastated San Francisco was a 7.9 on the Richter scale. 8.1 got their attention!

Mobile Billboards

Our next guerilla marketing technique was the design and production of a 22-foot long by 13-foot high super-photorealistic double-sided mobile billboard, which we placed at the foot of Market Street, directly across from San Francisco's iconic Ferry Building. The billboard was designed to fit within the natural visual perspective as one would see walking out of the Ferry Building, where thousands of commuters enter San Francisco each morning. The billboard was designed by Publicis & Hal Riney. Below is the original design concept, showing the perspective we wanted on downtown, and then the final mobile billboard in position. What confronted these early-morning commuters was a full color photo-realistic presentation of Market Street with an earthquake crack running right down the middle, buildings collapsing all around it, and sparks flying from downed electrical lines. It literally stopped people in their tracks.

The opposite side of this mobile billboard depicted the same earthquake crack running all the way up to the Ferry Building, showing overturned cars, a collapsing Ferry Building tower and the inside of the building engulfed in flames! If you were on Market Street, as many thousands were, on their way to work, this was their view when looking down the street toward the Ferry Building. On the following page is the original design concept and then the final billboard in position.

These billboards were so realistic you could almost smell the smoke and feel the fire.

Anyone who had a camera, cell phone or video recorder pulled it out and started taking pictures of these amazing billboards. We also positioned Red Cross volunteer videographers and photographers

Design concept of billboard placement

Final billboard in position with a perfect street/buildings perspective

around the area to capture the reactions of the people on the street, many of whom stood in stunned silence. It was shock and awe at its very (luckily non-lethal) best! We held the press conference adjacent to the mobile billboard and introduced the emergency preparedness campaign and the free trainings that the Red Cross was offering. This was

Design concept of billboard placement

Final billboard in position with a perfect Ferry Building perspective

the kickoff of an extraordinary series of promotional activities. Over the next two weeks, the mobile billboard was driven throughout the greater San Francisco area, stopping pedestrians and traffic wherever it went, while Red Cross volunteers passed out informational pamphlets about our free emergency preparedness training.

The Bay Area media jumped all over these in-your-face billboards and provided exceptional news coverage on local television and radio stations, newspapers and blogs. Of course, we also invited the wire services and other media outlets to visit the billboards, and we sent photos to our extensive media list.

Blogs and Wire Services

The blog community and wire services went especially wild, sending the photos of the mobile billboards all across the world. Of all the extraordinary media coverage, our favorite was a blog comment that stated: "When did the Red Cross get so cool?

China magazine story

England newspaper story

"Crashed" Taxicabs

A few weeks after our press conference and the unveiling of the mobile billboards, we put two "crashed" taxicabs into service in downtown San Francisco and downtown Oakland. These were real working cabs… with slight modifications! A decal was placed across the car providing "be prepared" website and contact information. Sitting prominently on the roof of these taxicabs was a fabricated pile of "rubble" supposedly from falling debris. While tens of thousands of people stood only a few feet away from this startling preparedness message, I'm not sure how many people actually got into the cabs themselves.

Outdoor Billboards and Bus Cards

Thanks to the generosity of Bay Area outdoor billboard companies, as well as the contacts and influence provided by Publicist & Hal Riney, we placed approximately 50 outdoor billboards and smaller posters (called bus cards) at bus stops all across the Bay Area, depicting famous San Francisco area landmarks "shaking" with the message of *Prepare Bay Area*. The only part of these posters in focus was the damaged sign, telephone number and website address. It was a very effective communication of our earthquake preparedness message.

Photos courtesy of American Red Cross

Publicity Campaign

By design, the primary focus of our media relations and publicity campaign was to generate free coverage through our extraordinary guerilla marketing techniques and events. Additionally, press information was continually distributed on the importance of preparing for an earthquake and encouraging people to visit the Red Cross website where they would find detailed information on developing an emergency kit, making a plan and signing up for CPR training.

We also received excellent coverage by placing Red Cross spokespersons on local community affairs radio and TV programming and many other media interview opportunities.

Wherever possible, we also delivered our campaign message in Spanish and Chinese.

Northern California Broadcasters Association

I was able to make a presentation to the Board of Directors of the Northern California Broadcasters Association and asked for their help and influence in supporting this campaign. In an unprecedented offering of paid advertising spots, the Northern California Broadcasters Association provided 3,300 30-second spots on 60 radio stations to support this campaign. These spots were not public service announcements, but rather actual advertisements that were placed in the normal daytime advertising rotation on their stations. The estimated value of this donation was nearly $700,000 of free advertising. This was the largest advertising donation I have ever seen in my career for a regional, cause-related campaign, and it was extraordinarily helpful in motivating people to get trained by the Red Cross.

Super Crack!

As they say on the infomercials: "But wait... there's more!" Never underestimate your creativity when you're on a roll. Several months later, to re-energize the media coverage and the public awareness of our *Prepare Bay Area* campaign, we held an event called Super Crack! Again utilizing the terrific creativity of our pro bono partners Publicis & Hal Riney, we designed and placed a 60' x 10' photorealistic decal across Union Square in downtown San Francisco. This decal made it look as if the world-famous Union Square had been cracked in half by an earthquake. As Union Square sits above a multi-story parking lot, the decal depicted a three-dimensional view, showing crumbling chunks of concrete which had fallen into the crack and smashed the cars below. To emphasize the "reality" of the devastation, we put yellow "Caution: Do Not Cross" security tape on stanchions surrounding the decal and had security personnel present to make sure that

Photos by Bruce Burtch

people didn't "fall" into the crack. We took television and wire service camera teams to the top of the Macy's building which overlooks Union Square so they could photograph and videotape Super Crack from its best perspective, looking down on Union Square.

As with the mobile billboards, the unique, in-your-face approach of Super Crack received strong media coverage in Bay Area media stations and far beyond.

As in any successful motivational campaign strategy, once you grab your audience's attention, you need to provide them with information you want them to use. In the case of Super Crack, our Red Cross training team and volunteers had set up tents and provided free emergency preparedness training throughout the week Super Crack was on Union Square.

Guerilla marketing techniques, which we utilized in this campaign, come in all sizes and types. When you realistically depict the destruction of major streets and landmark buildings, crack a famous public park in half and pile simulated rubble on top of actual working taxicabs - this is guerrilla marketing on steroids. However, as with any form of marketing, guerilla or otherwise, the message you are conveying must be on target with your campaign strategy. In this Red Cross example, our guerilla marketing strategy of "What will it take to get your attention?" was well executed and presented by visually attacking the complacency of San Francisco Bay Area residents unprepared for a major earthquake or other national disaster.

Campaign Results

Taken as a whole, the *Prepare Bay Area* campaign was an unqualified smash, so to speak. The campaign created tremendous public exposure and interaction and generated sensational news stories, wire photographs, viral and social media coverage and more which went all around the San Francisco Bay Area, across the country, and around the world. The pro bono creative and personnel donations alone from Publicis & Hal Riney easily exceeded $200,000.

However, no matter how creative a campaign may be, if it doesn't meet its objectives - it's a waste of time and money. This was not the case. The *Prepare Bay Area* campaign generated an astonishing three million dollars in free publicity and media coverage. Most importantly, the publicity and enormous word-of-mouth promotion motivated the training of over one million Bay Area residents in emergency preparedness - that means approximately 26% or more of all people living in the American Red Cross Bay Area chapter's four-county region. *Prepare Bay Area* was (and still is) the most successful nongovernmental emergency preparedness campaign in history.

Reflecting upon the success of *Prepare Bay Area*, PG&E's Erza Garrett commented, "Beyond the critical importance of preparing one million of our customers for an emergency - which of course includes our own employees, families, friends and loved ones – this program provided PG&E the opportunity to reinforce for our customers that we are focused on public safety and enabled our employees to work directly with their neighbors, in the communities where they live and work, to build their own personal preparedness plan."

The three-year campaign expenses for the marketing, publicity, creative and material production, not including our Red Cross marketing staff time, were approximately $100,000. Compared with smaller, more local cross-sector partnerships and cause marketing campaigns, such a sum may seem quite large. For a marketing campaign the magnitude of *Prepare Bay Area*, which received $3 million in free publicity and was undertaken in the sixth largest metropolitan area of the United States, it was an extraordinarily small amount. Due to the creative strategy, we were able to leverage the motivation and abilities of all of our partners to make this happen. I firmly believe that almost any campaign or program has the opportunity to attain a high level of success when the right partners come together and get creative, while focused on the greater good.

Prepare Bay Area 2.0

The clearest indication of a successful cross-sector partnership campaign is when all partners want to continue their relationship. Following the extraordinary success of *Prepare Bay Area*, Pacific Gas & Electric and the American Red Cross Bay Area chapter again teamed up in 2010 to expand the preparedness program through the Ready Neighborhoods Initiative. Ready Neighborhoods is designed to transform communities throughout Northern and Central California into models of disaster readiness. As Ezra Garrett explained, "The tremendous results on multiple fronts that were delivered by *Prepare Bay Area* provided strong motivation for us to look for opportunities to extend this success by 1) deepening our impact within the Bay Area, and 2) scaling the program out beyond the Bay Area across the state. As the gas and electric utility provider for northern and central California, we serve one in twenty Americans, so the ability to scale is a very important factor as we assess partnership opportunities."

For this expanded initiative, PG&E donated $2.5 million to the Red Cross, two and a half times their initial funding of the original *Prepare Bay Area* campaign.

Rejoice, Revise and Repeat
The Debrief

Shortly after the end of the first phase or first year of the project or campaign, while all the successes and challenges are still fresh in each partner's mind, bring your entire partnership team together and do an analysis/debrief on every aspect of the partnership, the project or campaign, the successes and the shortcomings. This meeting should have a predetermined agenda to be sure that you will cover all the important areas. I suggest you cover the following areas at the minimum:

- Did you meet the overriding partnership objectives as established in your original partnership assessment, creative and tactical strategies, Written Agreement, Marketing Plan and other aspects of the effort?

- What was your ROI, in other words what specifically did you accomplish as to the amount of money raised, people served, project built on time, etc.?

- If you didn't meet all of your goals, looking back do you feel the standards were set too high?

- Was anything left out because of a lack of time, lack of resources, or for other reasons?

- Did all the partners fulfill their individual responsibilities?

- Did the individual organizations work together as an integrated partnership team?

- If sponsors or outside organizations were involved (such as pro bono agencies, sponsors for specific events, etc., did they meet the expectations of the partnership? Did they fulfill their contractual relationships, if applicable?

- Did the volunteers fulfill their responsibilities?

- Were the volunteers managed for success so that they could maximize their effectiveness?

- What went wrong?

- What really amazed you?

- What would you like to change going forward into a Phase 2, second year or other progression of the partnership?

- Moving forward, would you like to add new partners, and if so, who?

This is not a time to point fingers and blame people; it is a time to make sure that you have an accurate and candid report on all the key aspects of the campaign or project. The answers to these questions and more should be written down into a final report which can be reviewed by the individual partners and key stakeholders. It serves both as a comprehensive wrap-up and sets the foundation for what comes next. This debrief must not be overlooked – no matter what happened.

Rejoice

Put a closing stamp on this project or campaign and that stamp should be one of rejoicing! After all, this entire effort was about serving the individual and mutual goals of the partners and to serve the greater good...and there's just not enough rejoicing about such important service. So it's time to party!! Get your team together and all others who were integral to the success of your campaign. Go out to dinner in a neutral location, somewhere fun, and as far away from the workaday world as possible. This is a great time for some zany rewards, such as a prize for the person who came up with the craziest idea, a volunteer who offered the most time, the one who talked too much at the meetings (I always win that one!), etc. I don't recommend plaques or trophies...unless they are humorous. Make this stuff fun.

In addition to these fun internal awards, now is the time to go after some serious recognition. I guarantee you that your pro bono public relations or advertising agency will want to submit their work for industry awards and you want to encourage them to do just that, and support their submissions. If there are awards within the industry or nonprofit areas of your partners - go after these also. Absolutely contact your local press, Chambers of Commerce, nonprofit associations, industry newsletters, and other forms of press and communications and give them the facts and figures of your successful project or campaign. (Of course, you should have been giving them updates all along the process.) Be sure to promote the success and involvement of all the partners, and any outside funders, sponsors, supporters, suppliers, etc. that helped you achieve your success.

This is not just tooting your own horn. Everyone likes and deserves to be recognized for a job well done. In many cases this recognition will attract the interest of new partners, the media and other important stakeholders who might want to join you as you move into the next phase. Everyone likes to jump on the bandwagon that's playing the song of success. Take advantage of this opportunity.

The primary goal of *Win-Win for the Greater Good* is to provide you with a guidebook on the most efficient, most effective, most proven ways to have your organization and your partnership stand out to all your audiences for the good work you are doing for them and for the greater good. Your organization will not glow unless people know and see what you are doing. So shine those spotlights!

Revise and Repeat

After the emotional (and possibly literal) hangover from all this partying and recognition, you will find yourself in one of three places:

1) Your campaign was a blow-out success - congratulations! Start planning for next year.

Set a date in the very near future to bring the partnership team back together and discuss moving forward into the next phase. If your partnership was focused on a particular project such as building a new homeless shelter, what might you do next to serve the homeless in your community or beyond? The most successful cross-sector partnerships do not hit their stride until the second or third year. The Campbell's Soup/Kroger Foods/Susan G. Komen partnership doubled their sales/donations in their second year. Safeway's relationship with Easter Seals is 25 years and growing.

2) You did not fully meet your expectations, but the partnership sees strong potential in moving forward to develop a follow-up campaign.

Your debrief uncovered areas for improvement, but overall you felt that it was a good partnership with positive results, and you know you could do even better next year. You have the strong advantage of knowing what worked and what didn't work. Your success may have attracted new partners and new stakeholders. Certainly ideas came up during the first campaign that might work better in the second or third year with more experience under your collective belt. Partnerships are not for the timid. Success comes through trial and error, but mostly when you keep your eye focused on increasing your efforts for the greater good.

3) You decided, for whatever reasons, to call it quits after this one project or campaign.

Okay, stuff happens. Fortunately, it doesn't happen that often. Personal chemistry plays a big part in failed partnerships. If the people don't work well together, the partnership is doomed, at least in most cases. If you must call it quits, still hold the debrief session and maybe the party. There is much you can learn from this experience that could be of service to you in other aspects of your business and future partnerships. You never know when you will run into these partners again, need to ask for advice or possibly provide an introduction to some other organization. So, if you must end the partnership, end on as high a note as possible.

Scaling Your Success

Assuming you do not call it quits, but have your first success under your belts, the partnership has built trust and confidence in taking on a major challenge and the knowledge that as a well-oiled team machine, you can accomplish just about anything. Joining along with you is a strong support system of energized individuals or team members who want to ride this wagon of success, media who want to see what you will do next (and cover it) and a community ready to lend a hand. So why stop here?

Building one homeless shelter or any first project or campaign for that matter is just the tip of the proverbial iceberg. You may wish to build additional shelters or initiate pet adoption drives, a HIV/AIDS awareness campaign, afterschool programs, youth art installations, and so much more in your city, county, state or across the country, depending on the size and scope of your operation. Organizations like Habitat for Humanity and Rebuilding Together have formed national partnerships with well-aligned for-profit organizations such as Sears, Whirlpool, Home Depot, Bank of America and Lowe's, who are working together on multiple projects in multiple locations.

You don't need to be a major for-profit or nonprofit to expand your partnership to other locations or greater achievements.

As you are beginning to develop your creative and operational strategy to scale your success, pull together everything you developed as part of your campaign: every proposal, graphic design, press release, budget, your creative and tactical strategies, Written Agreement, photographs, video clips, volunteer strategy, partner descriptions, Marketing Plan, media coverage, debrief session report, etc., cataloguing what went right and what went wrong. At the very least, this compilation will serve as an excellent record of your project or campaign to be shared with all partners and all stakeholders. At best, it serves as your solid foundation and blueprint for your next, possibly even greater cross-sector partnership accomplishment.

You Are Beginning to Glow!

If you read this book in preparation for beginning your exploration of a cross-sector partnership project or campaign, my hope is that you can now envision the beneficial effect this campaign will have on your organization, your partners, your stakeholders and yourself. I hope you can see how others will be attracted to your campaign because of the greater good you are seeking to achieve. Of course you can! And as you start to see the success and feel this attractiveness, you and all involved in your organization will begin to radiate confidence and a sense of accomplishment of having done something really well that serves others in need - the greater good. You must feel it...for you are beginning to **glow**.

The more you are focused on having all of the partners and stakeholders benefiting from this project or campaign, the brighter that glow will become. It may begin subtly, as in the pride and positive tone in the voice of your CEO in answering questions from a TV reporter, or in the laughter of your colleagues recalling a particularly funny situation that came up when volunteering for this project, or the lump in your throat when the doors opened and a homeless family entered the shelter for their only meal of the day - a shelter you helped build. As these tiny, seemingly insignificant moments of emotion and pride begin to swell up and bond together, your organization and each partner will start to glow even brighter, and this glow will meet its zenith when your world, be it local, regional or national, recognizes what you have done together in partnership for the greater good.

Whether you are a for-profit organization that has embedded a cause consciousness deep within your corporate culture or the non-profit, education or government partner that is the recipient of the partnership's efforts, your organization will stand apart from all of your competition. Your employees' satisfaction levels will rise, the best employees will want to work with you, new investors or donors will want to engage with you, your brand will shine, your organization will grow, your community will sing your praises and new partners will bring you innovative and exciting ideas.

The grand opportunity is not just to achieve this glow but to maintain the glow, and in time, increase its brightness and its attractiveness to your organization. Bask in this glow, revel in its brilliance, and appreciate that your hard work, long hours and deep commitment led to this magical feeling. Like moths to a flame, this attractiveness, this glow, will draw new opportunities, new challenges and new successes.

Maintaining Glow

You must be vigilant and not let the glow fade—you have too much to lose. For once you have achieved this internal and external state of glow, every fiber in your being will want to continue moving forward, seeking new ways to benefit those who need your help. Whether you continue on the path of your first project or campaign, expanding its benefit and reach, or venture down new roads of partnership, new areas of opportunity to explore, you must do so well-prepared. You now have all that it takes to achieve and act upon your personal and organizational foundation of cause consciousness.

There is so much that needs to be done. And you are ready. So go forth, and glow brightly!

Epilogue

Her name was Jill. She taught me more about courage, determination, overcoming obstacles, and the sheer joy of participation than anyone I ever met.

In the early 80's my public relations firm was providing pro bono services for the Special Olympics California State Games. Everything was going rather well, so I decided to walk around and check out some of the competitions. I just happened to go over to the 25-yard dash that was about to start for the most physically-challenged (in addition to being mentally-challenged) athletes at the Special Olympics games.

There were about 10 young men and women lined up, all eagerly anticipating the firing of the starter's pistol. When the shot rang out, off they went in speeds, ranging from pretty fast - especially one fellow on crutches who was really moving - to others who were struggling just to walk. Quickly the first athlete (the guy on crutches) passed the finish line to the screams and hugs of everyone watching the race. He was followed over the next several seconds by the rest of the athletes, all except one.

Back near the starting line sat a young woman in a wheelchair, and she was just about 4 feet from the starting line. Jill was so physically challenged that she was bent completely over in her wheelchair. Her head was about a foot above her lap and she couldn't use her left arm, but her right hand was on the large wheel of her wheelchair and her eyes were staring straight down the track. She could only move the wheel one stretch of her right hand. So I imagine she went about eight to 10 inches down the track with each challenging motion of that hand. When I looked at her face, she had the most amazingly determined expression I have ever seen.

As you can imagine, all the athletes and visitors who were watching this particular event started to whoop and holler and cheer for this courageous young woman. She would move her hand one movement and stop, then move it again, and stop... so slowly, methodically, moving down the track. The noise from the people surrounding that part of the track grew so loud and so sustained that it attracted the attention of nearly everyone in the stadium. In a matter of minutes, there were hundreds of people surrounding that short piece of track, surrounding Jill and cheering her on. And slowly, her hand continued moving that wheel about eight to 10 inches with each turn.

I don't remember how long it took Jill to reach the finish line. It could've been seven minutes, it could've been 10. We were all so caught up in the courage of her effort that time didn't exist. Everyone was screaming encouragement, and nearly everyone, including myself, was crying, overwhelmed by emotion. When she finally crossed the finish line, the entire stadium erupted in pandemonium and Jill was mobbed. You should have seen her smile.

I have been to many Special Olympics meets over the years and to many sporting events at all levels, including the International Olympic Games, but I have never witnessed such a triumph or seen such an athlete like Jill.

I know it's tough out there. So the next time you face any challenge in your cross-sector partnership, cause marketing, business, nonprofit or personal efforts, let Jill be your inspiration. I want you to feel her determination and receive the gift that she continues to give to us all. Because you can't tell Jill that she's not going to finish that race. You can't tell Jill that it's just too hard. You can't tell Jill that she's not special, because she is. Jill is the greater good.

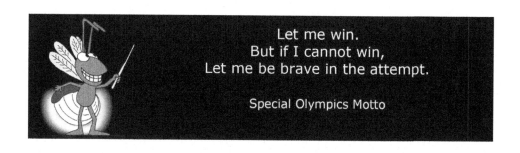

Let me win.
But if I cannot win,
Let me be brave in the attempt.

Special Olympics Motto

About the Author

Called the "Father of Cause Marketing" by the Cause Marketing Forum, Bruce Burtch is recognized as a pioneer and international expert in the field of cross-sector partnerships and cause marketing. Bruce builds highly innovative partnerships among the nonprofit, for-profit, education and government sectors, which maximize their strategic marketing, revenue development and brand-building success. He has served as Public Affairs Manager with Marriott Corporation, Public Relations Director for the United States Olympic Committee, VP and General Manager of Schulberg Mediaworks, Director of Marketing and Communications for the American Red Cross Bay Area chapter, and served as Consultant to the President of Xerox Global Services. Bruce founded The William Bentley Agency, the first integrated marketing agency in the San Francisco Bay Area.

In 2010, Bruce founded a highly-specialized consultancy, Bruce W. Burtch, Inc., to focus on the area of his greatest interest: creating cross-sector partnerships and cause marketing campaigns between nonprofit, for-profit, education and government sectors, with the focus of creating a greater good. Bruce is also Executive Director of 10,000 Partnerships™, a nonprofit organization which provides training workshops in cross-sector partnerships.

Bruce is credited with designing the first cause marketing campaign: a partnership between March of Dimes and Marriott Corporation in 1976. He designed and directed the American Red Cross Prepare Bay Area cause marketing campaign which motivated the unprecedented training of over one million San Francisco Bay Area residents in emergency preparedness, while garnering three million dollars in free publicity.

Bruce was awarded the Distinguished Leadership Award, presented by the National Association of Community Leadership, for spearheading the development of the Tenderloin After-School Program, in San Francisco. While still an undergraduate, Bruce conceived the nation's only degree-granting college, based on England's Oxford-Cambridge tutorial system, the nationally-acclaimed Honors Tutorial College at Ohio University.

Bruce W. Burtch, Inc. provides consulting, training and speaking services which motivate win-win partnerships focused on creating a greater good.

I want to Hear From You!

If you have followed the guidelines, case studies and suggestions in this book and from our online **Resource Center**, you now know more about developing cross-sector partnerships and cause marketing than most. Take advantage of this amazing opportunity to do good and to glow. It is my sincere hope that you will let me know about the partnerships you have developed. Please contact me directly at *bruce@bruceburtch.com*, and share your good news!

Made in the USA
Middletown, DE
06 March 2020